Trend
Following
Mindset

Also by Michael W. Covel

*Trend Following: How to Make a Fortune in
Bull, Bear, and Black Swan Markets*

*The Complete TurtleTrader: How 23 Novice Investors
Became Overnight Millionaires*

*The Little Book of Trading: Trend Following
Strategy for Big Winnings*

*Trend Commandments: Trading
for Exceptional Returns*

Trend Following Mindset

The Genius of Legendary Trader Tom Basso

Michael W. Covel

Harriman House

HARRIMAN HOUSE LTD

3 Viceroy Court

Bedford Road

Petersfield

Hampshire

GU32 3LJ

GREAT BRITAIN

Tel: +44 (0)1730 233870

Email: enquiries@harriman-house.com

Website: harriman.house

First published in 2021.

Hardback ISBN: 978-0-85719-814-3

eBook ISBN: 978-0-85719-815-0

British Library Cataloguing in Publication Data

A CIP catalogue record for this book can be obtained from the British Library.

Thank you for everything Liễu Trịnh

Contents

Living with "Mr. Serenity"— Foreword by Brenda Russell-Basso

I MET Tom one week after he had retired, when we both attended a two-step dance lesson in Scottsdale, AZ. This was not in some upscale venue; it was in a cowboy dive bar. Upon leaving, I noticed that Tom drove a rather unremarkable SUV, which he later described as a utilitarian, 12-year-old vehicle. After seeing each other intermittently over a few months of lessons, the two of us had more conversations. I soon learned that Tom was avidly putting together, with dedication and energy, a retirement life to include all his many interests. I later realized this dedication and energy was a carry-over from his long career. The interests are many. Besides dancing there is golf, singing, cooking, painting, fishing, landscaping, reading, and wine-making. Such a combination of time use may put a question mark on any type of serenity, but as I got to know Tom, I began to understand.

Fast forward to one of Tom's recent seminars on trading, where I was the moderator. At a break, one of the participants casually asked me what it was like to live with "Mr. Serenity," that famous moniker bestowed on Tom by Jack Schwager. After a couple of comments, we had drawn a small crowd. Apparently, this topic is of more interest than I would have thought. If you read interviews with Tom and study his methodology and long success in trading, you would probably accurately think, "I don't want to be in that head." Retirement could be hectic and stressful, trying to conscientiously include all the elements. Delving further, though, you would understand that he applies that same focused but non-stressed attitude in retirement that he applied in his work life. He constructs his "movie of life" to suit himself, and each interest is compartmentalized and enjoyed in a relaxed fashion.

There is, however, evidence of his analytical, engineer mind that he applied so meticulously to designing trading strategies with detailed execution. When Tom was 12, he bought a book on hypnotizing oneself to sleep. I am a witness: he can put himself to sleep in about six seconds. Once when working on his golf swing, he remarked, "I think I need to get 30% more weight on my left side." And when people ask about the kind of dog we have, our chill rescue Banjo, Tom answers every time: "25% miniature poodle, 25% miniature schnauzer, and 50% terrier mix with probably a lot of wheaten due to his color." (Mixed breed, rescue might suffice.)

A recipe he invents has a pinch of this, a dash of that, and some varied and unexpected components that usually result in a tasty concoction most could not imagine. (I am the lucky sampler.) He is a compendium of information on 70s rock and roll, and can recognize most hits and the artists in the first few seconds. (I prefer Beethoven myself.) And imagine my surprise when I found out he had a detailed list of 20 traits he would look for in a possible mate. (Luckily, I somehow hit 19.5 of those. The other half point? I will never be 5'9" tall.) His mind does focus on details. A friend of ours is fond of saying, "Don't ask Tom what time it is, because he will tell you how to build a watch!"

But let's go back to the serenity topic. I don't often ask how our portfolios are doing. I handle our real estate investments and don't cross over into trading. On occasion though, I will say, "Did we make any money today?" A response could be, "No. We lost ____ dollars." I feel I need to choke and pound my chest, but the news is delivered in a matter-of-fact, non-emotional manner. Likewise, if the answer is that we made a rather large profit, I feel like applauding and perhaps clicking heels. However, again the response from Tom is the same—matter of fact with no discernible reaction. I have learned that he truly lives one of his favorite sayings: "The market will do what the market will do."

The answer to that student's question is that living with Mr. Serenity is serene indeed in every aspect. I get to see up close how Tom moves through his "to-do lists" with calm purpose. We don't have volatility in our life together. Basically, we just "enjoy the ride" every day.

Brenda Russell-Basso

Preface

"So bad. Ranting nonsense. This is brutal. This guy has issues and uses this podcast as a therapy session. Pure, pure garbage."

This is one of my all-time favorite reviews of my Trend Following podcast (www.trendfollowing.com/podcast).

The podcast is now at 1000+ episodes, 10 million listens, and includes six Nobel Prize winners, multiple billionaires, and an untold number of world-class entrepreneurs and academics. But I am honored that one guy felt compelled to write his anger, because a podcast like mine is not for everyone (more on that in a second).

You want to start listening now? That will take you over four weeks of continuous listening, 24/7!

What have I learned from all of these great podcast guests? What are some common themes? Six come to mind:

1. Do the right thing, and let the chips fall where they may.
2. Talking about a guest's natural talent is undermining their hard work and dedication to their craft.
3. Know the difference between skill and luck.
4. A lot of people don't like the truth.
5. Process over outcome is how you get ahead.
6. There is a good chance you won't ever know *why*, so follow the trend.

Now I might not have Joe Rogan's or Tim Ferriss's mega listens (yet), but I am always amazed that a podcast gives such reach. A guy, a microphone and Skype or Zoom broadcasting from parts unknown with word of mouth viral as the driver? Amazing. What a fun time to be alive.

What's the craziest way someone found my podcast? I can thank comedian and *Seinfeld* co-creator Larry David:

"It's funny how I started listening to you. I was looking for podcasts with Larry David and I found the one you did about *Curb Your Enthusiasm*. From that, my investing has taken a major change of course. I now have my kids checking you if I listen to a podcast I think they would relate to. But I don't force it on them. They will figure out what is best for them."

Isn't that awesome? The small world in action.

So how does a podcast like this start? Great guests. And I am lucky to have those. But it did not start out of the gate with great guests. It was a slow build—literally years. However, one guest in particular helped put my podcast into motion back in 2012. Let me let another reader introduce that guest as he talks about my episode 400:

"I said to myself, 'There's no way in hell I'm listening to a four-hour episode with **Tom Basso** ...' And then I got to hour three and said to myself, 'I owe you an apology, holy **** this is amazing.'"

Let me back up.

Tom Basso was originally featured in Jack Schwager's *Market Wizards* series and is most famously known as "Mr. Serenity." Now retired from managing client money, Tom was president and founder of Trendstat Capital Management. He became a registered investment advisor in 1980 and a registered commodities advisor in 1984. He has deep experience in trend following trading. He's a living legend.

No surprise I pursued him for his first podcast interview and he graciously agreed. Then he came on the podcast again, and again and again. The reception? The enthusiasm for Tom *the retired legend* was tremendous. What was it about Tom that resonated? His *mindset*. Meat and potatoes. Blunt. To the point, but caring. This is a unique way of being.

Then, one day I said to myself, "What if I added all of Tom's episodes together to create one mega episode?" That became my episode 400. Mega episode 400 became an instant hit, but it did not stop there. Tom came on again and again. People loved him, so being the wise broadcaster, I listened to my audience.

What's special about Tom Basso?
What makes his voice one you must consider?

Most investors attempt to study supply and demand, or some other fundamental factor they believe underlies some market value. They rely on government policy, economic projections, price-earnings ratios, and balance sheet analysis to make their buy and sell decisions. It's a religion. And that religion (or cult) is called fundamental analysis. It boils down to telling stories—the stuff you see across Bloomberg, CNBC, etc., 24/7. It's all a big guessing game. It's an ego game.

Turn all of that off. I want you to think differently. I want you to think like Tom Basso—the trend follower. My objective with *Trend Following Mindset* is simple: combine all I can find about Tom in one unique book. That means all of my interviews (and others), plus Tom's most important trend following research papers.

An associate I have known for a long time pitched me on a new guest for my podcast.

She: "Do you have a template of questions you want to pass on to him?"

Me: "No."

Before jumping into my first interview with Tom, I want to say something about my interview philosophy. A good interview doesn't ask questions. It's a conversation. I don't ask topical questions about current events—that's pointless. Headline interviews are brain poison for newbies who want to lose all of their money. I want timeless, universal insights from my guests. And what follows is just that— my timeless conversations with Tom (in Part 1), plus detailed insights about trading pulled from Tom's career research (Part 2).

Author Seth Godin once said, "Once a commitment is made to a streak, the question shifts from, 'Should I blog tomorrow?' to, 'What will tomorrow's blog say?'"

That's exactly how I view my books and podcast. And I am damn lucky that a guy like Tom Basso helped to launch my podcast and ultimately *Trend Following Mindset*. Now it's up to you. Take Tom's market wisdom, his making money wisdom, or not. **Your choice.**

* * *

To receive my free interactive trend following presentation send a picture of your receipt to receipt@trendfollowing.com.

PART I
Interviews

Enjoy the Ride

EPISODE 10: APRIL 25, 2012

Tom Basso: This is the first interview I've done in about eight years since I retired.

Michael Covel: I find that in trend trading, experience doesn't have a half-life; it doesn't go away. There's a lot of wisdom that we can all pick up from folks that have been down the dusty trail. I sometimes hear people telling me, "Oh, Covel, what are you going to learn from these guys from decades ago?" My response is always along the lines of, "Eh, are you serious?"

Tom: Not much changes, Michael. It's the same thing. I was just looking today to make sure I knew where everything was, since I haven't been interviewed in so long. I just did a Google search on my name and TrendStat, my old firm's name, and I was amazed at what I found … I gave up after 30 pages of results. It was amazing to see all the information that stays on the web. Once it's on there it stays there forever, so I had a trip down memory lane.

Michael: Let's start with your younger days. A lot of people want to know, "What was Tom Basso like at 13 or 16?" What were you thinking about? What were you doing early on, and how did the migration happen, the switch?

Tom: When I was 12 years old, I delivered papers—the *Syracuse Herald-Journal*—in the evenings. I had about 82 subscribers and made about $10 a week. Around that time, a mutual fund salesman showed up at my dad's house. I listened in to their conversation, got interested in what I heard, and then started buying mutual funds.

Michael: 12! That's a head start.

Tom: By the time I got to college, I had gotten back to break-even on that position, due to the amount of fees the salesman was taking out of the front end. I was about 18 years old, and I was just breaking even on the funds. It was then that I realized the markets went up and down. In junior year of college I started worrying about where was I going to get a job as a chemical engineer—which is what I graduated in from Clarkson University up in Potsdam, New York.

I had about 25 different job offers, so I thought one way to look at this might be to plot the stock of some of these companies, and take a look at what they did. I ended up going to work for Monsanto in St. Louis. I plotted Monsanto's stock and ended up trading Monsanto because it went up and down. I realized that it'd be foolish to just buy and hold it because it seemed to pop up to 40 and go down to 20. I figured I'd might as well make money each time it does that because it didn't seem to get much above 40 in those days. I'm talking back in the '70s.

That led me more to trying to quantify, "How do I do this without having to think too much about it?" Because I was a busy guy. I was getting an MBA, working as a chemical engineer, and starting up with the original firm that was the precursor of TrendStat, called Kennedy Capital. And actually, Kennedy Capital still exists today in St. Louis as a small cap manager. I sold my share at Kennedy Capital and started TrendStat. It was an evolution getting into futures and currencies using trend following techniques. I ran out of futures capacity. One thing leads to another and pretty soon 28 years have gone by, and I'm retiring.

Michael: Guys like yourself, you tell that whole story really fast, about 30 seconds. I'm not going to let you off the hook that quick. Beyond your own internal studies and looking at charts and observing this up and down nature of trends, were you inspired or influenced by anybody that came before you?

Tom: Not really. I was an engineer by background, and was very good with computers, but you've got to realize that I never was a broker. I never worked at an investment bank. Never was on the floor of any exchange. I really started out managing other people's money by way of an investment club. A lot of the investment club people were lazy, and they left it to two of us to do most of the work. I was one of those two guys.

Having been an engineer by background gave me a real heavy dosage of math, logic, problem-solving, and how to do things efficiently. I began to see human endeavor categorized in two camps. There was the production side of things where you're grinding out something that you could teach a computer to do, but for some reason you've decided to do it as a human being. And the other side of human endeavor is more the creative side: The side where you can't really teach a computer how to create something new—a piece of art or whatever.

I realized that I had a limited amount of time. If I was ever going to be creative and take trading to a new level by reading new books and exploring new research angles, I had to get the actual trading function: The buying and selling. Where am I going to buy and where am I going to sell? How much am I going to buy and how much am I going to sell?

I had to get those functions to a point where it was so cookbook I could get it done in very short amounts of time so that I'd have time left to do the creative things I enjoy.

You remember the RadioShack TRS-80? That was the first computer I got. I went from there to the IBM PC and bought an AT after that. I just kept programming and programming. My sole purpose was to just put myself out of work in terms of trading every day. I evolved my trading into a very, very automated TrendStat Capital that basically made no decisions by human beings day after day. It was a highly automated operation covering some 80 futures markets, 30 currency markets and about 20 mutual funds that we traded by many different strategies and many different dollars. It was quite complicated, but we would just buy another computer, and crank our system into it.

Michael: You're self-taught. You are on the outside. You are not a part of the trading floor up in New York City somewhere. You're not on the exchange floor. Talk to me about when it hit you that, "There's all these guys out there doing fundamentals." Warren Buffett, for example, is a value guy. But you've made the decision that you're going to use prices as your core variable, and you're going to start to code this.

This was all the buying and selling of price as a variable and figuring out how much to bet. That was something that you were figuring out on your own by trial and error without any outside influences?

Tom: I started looking at some of my early stuff that I did, like my mutual fund purchase with the mutual fund salesman, and other purchases of actual stock after that. I looked a little bit at fundamentals and realized it was a quagmire of accounting information to get through. It took too much time.

I realized that no matter what I did it seemed like there was always going to be somebody with a lot more time and staffs of people. I had other engineers at Monsanto, and we'd be sitting there in lunch and they'd say, "What makes you think you can do any better than some Wall Street firm with teams of analysts figuring all this stuff out?" I got to thinking about *that* and started getting more global and distant from it all. When you take a step back and look at what these other guys do, you realize that everything these people do ends up somehow in a battle.

I imagined going back to the Waterloo days and you've got Napoleon and Wellington up on the hills watching their armies down in the valley. And then you could watch the frontline going to the left or going to the right depending on who's winning at any one point in time. I thought that was a good picture for what goes on in a market. There're lots of people doing lots of different things, and some of them are buying, and some of them are selling, and they all think they're right. They all think they know what they're doing, and they're doing it for a reason.

But the sum total of all of that is where the price ends up. Or in the case of the battle, where the frontline is. So I thought, "Well if I could chart this, then I would know where everybody that's participating wants to put this price, and if I just watch, I can see that the battle is being won by one side over the other." In other words, "If the buyers are beating the sellers this time around, then I might as well lean that way because it looks like they are winning the battle. If the sellers are winning the battle, it'd probably be good to go that way." I never think much more about it than that. That's still my thinking for what I do in everyday life, even up to today.

Michael: I caught an email exchange that you had with Ed Seykota a few years back. You were commenting on the fact that on his questions and answers page somebody had made the comment, "Tom Basso doesn't like much heat." Could you explain to novices *that* term. You responded to Seykota, and you said, "Well, hold on. It's not necessarily *that*, but I am giving clients what they can handle."

Tom: Exactly. One of the biggest areas where I found fault with a lot of money managers in my era, in the early going, is this concept that Ed calls "heat." I just call it how much risk you are putting into the portfolio. I think risk can be measured by a lot of different approaches. The ones that I used were specifically a percent of equity of the risks of the stop loss. So take your risk from where you are to wherever the stop is. That's one form of risk as a percent of equity.

The next one is volatility. How fast does a market move up or down each day as a percent of your equity? The third picks up weird guys like euro dollars—or in the old days some high margin, low volatility types of instruments that every now and again go crazy. If you have too much of them in the portfolio, you're taking on too much risk. Markets are smart enough to add the margin in there, so I had margin as a percent of equity.

I would do all three of those calculations and take whichever one came out the lowest in terms of number of contracts, and that was how many I did. So I always erred to the conservative side—the least number of contracts, the least amount of exposure. By doing that, I didn't draw attention to myself in terms of clients looking at things every day and being overly caffeinated. Clients weren't calling me every other hour saying, "Did you see what gold did today?" That was not going to serve the client well because they're basically going to always be excited when it's up and distraught when it's down.

I was trying to level up the psychology of my clients and make sure my own psychology was level. I didn't want to get excited either. That's why Jack picked up on the Mr. Serenity thing, I guess. Everything in my trading life every day was somewhat boring.

Michael: You talked about the desire to make sure clients could stand the heat, but you would approach your own portfolio differently.

People might hear you say this and think, "Okay, you're helping clients one way, but you're willing to do something else for your own portfolio." Maybe you can explain that differential? I'm assuming you meant you were willing to have a little more volatility and take more risk?

Tom: Exactly right. I understand exactly what I'm doing, and I understand where my risks are. I can scenario analysis to death anything I think might happen and feel like I can live with what I'm doing.

Take, as a good example, my mother who's 83 and has less than $100,000 to her name in terms of retirement and IRAs. She's going to sit there with zero knowledge. She almost is confused by what a CD at a bank is; that's the level of knowledge that she's got. So it's the opposite end of the spectrum. When I start talking about anything financial, her eyes glaze over, and she has no idea what I'm saying. I try to put myself in the position of my clients and what they feel comfortable with. As a money manager you're being paid to manage other people's money so one of your first questions has to be, "What are my clients all going to look like, and how can I provide them something that I think that they will hire me for and keep me on the books for a long period of time?"

Otherwise, a lot of CTAs in the past, especially, could do 50% in a year, and then they'd lose 20%, and then they'd go 60% up and then another 27% down. They're all over the map. Their attitude is, "I'm going to trade the way I think is best to trade to make the most amount of money over the long run, and if you want to come along for a ride with me, you're welcome to, Mr. Client."

I approached it the other way around. I said, "I'm willing to sort of harness myself down a little bit because my job is to be a money manager. I need to be thinking about what my clients are looking for, not what I might want to do myself, because they're not prepared to do what I would do."

Michael: I'm guessing that you saved yourself quite a bit of grief. I'm not criticizing any of the guys that took the big risk and did the 50% up and 25% down, but I'm sure they heard from their clients a lot more in a negative way.

Tom: Oh and they had money coming in and out. They'd raise $100 million, and then they'd go down to $50 million, and then they're up to $250 million and then down to $100 million. I've got to believe they must be hiring people, firing people. It must be a chaotic way to run a business.

Michael: I wanted to jump into psychology—the psychology of trading in particular—because I have a feeling that this is where a lot of the success lies. And whether you're just a flat out entrepreneur, or a trader, the psychology of how you can make it through each day.

Tom: I agree. It's the most important thing in investing. It's way ahead of the second most important thing, which would be risk control, volatility control and basically all your money management side. It is way ahead of the importance of what everybody concentrates on—doing simulations on buy-sell decision models. That's the least important thing to worry about.

Michael: For the vast majority of folks out there, they still love that attitude.

Tom: The reason's easy to see. I've done studies that have been published, and there have been other studies way beyond what I did where you take markets, do a random number generator to buy or sell, put a good stop loss behind it, do good money management with it and you get a positive return on investment. If you're flipping a coin to buy and sell, how important can the buy and sell decision model be if you've put good money management behind it and you end up over time making a slight amount of money with a reasonable amount of risk?

But even more so than that, think about the psychology. A lot of people used to think of TrendStat and Tom Basso as a sort of robotic firm. Like we didn't think or we didn't do anything. But in reality I'm the guy that owns the company. Any moment I want to, I can change any of those black boxes that we're running.

If I don't have good psychology, don't understand what I'm doing, understand what buttons of mine are tending to be pushed with certain types of market action, things could go bad. If I stay the course and know that certain market action is normal or I know that something else is not normal, and I need to do some work on it, then I need to understand myself and the psychology that's being thrown into my face and my brain.

If I don't, I'm lost. I could change the models every day if I wanted to just because of the computers.

The psychology is the most important thing of all. That will drive what everybody does. It forces people to abandon systems that are basically sound systems. Just because a system is on a slight drawdown, traders start tweaking things, they overcomplicate things or they overly simplify things. Or they get on a run and get full of themselves and start leveraging too much, and then they blow up. There are a lot of different ways it can hit you, but understanding yourself is the most important thing of all.

Michael: When you say "understand yourself," tell me about Tom getting upset or Tom not getting upset. Did you go through your whole trading career on kind of an even keel? Were there ups and downs emotionally?

Tom: I was trading silver after being in the business maybe four or five years. My mom and dad were going to come and visit me down in St. Louis, which is where we were at that time. As the dutiful son, I take off the one week from trading and played tour guide. I was working as a chemical engineer, running them around, and consequently didn't have time to update my stuff. I missed a silver trade that broke out but, being the good, disciplined trader that I am, decided, "No, breakout already happened. Not going to jump in late." When I updated all my stuff after my mom and dad had left, I just missed it.

That turned out to be the most profitable trade of any market during the entire year. It was very frustrating watching it, and I realized that I needed to make sure that didn't happen again, because I didn't want to be frustrated like that. I told myself, "If I'm going to create a strategy, I have to be able to run it every single day, day after day, and not miss anything."

And I haven't missed a trade after that for years and years and years, because I put things in place. I put backups in place, and I make sure things are on stops. Whatever I have to do to make sure if I'm going to be, say, talking to you and markets will be open, or if I'm taking a vacation, everything will be taken care of. I'm going to Italy this summer. I'll be there three weeks, and I'll be trading right through it, and it won't bother me a bit. I'll still be on vacation.

Michael: I think for a lot of people, maybe if they're in that situation, instead of turning around and saying, "Oh, let's automate the approach," they would get upset about it. Sounds like you weren't emotionally upset. It was more of a problem to solve?

Tom: It was like an engineer's problem to solve. Think of it as a chemical factory. You've got stuff coming in one side, you process it, and it goes out the other side. And a lot of trading I thought of as chemical engineering too. You've got information coming in over satellite, com links and internet lines, and everything else. You process it either manually with your eyes and your brain, or by computer with databases and programming language—like we did at TrendStat. Then out come orders that are shipped off to exchanges, brokers, FCMs, and wherever they're going.

TrendStat to me was my little chemical factory. And when I look at the early days of my trading, I thought of it the same way. I've got a lot of information, I've got to get it done every day. I don't have a whole lot of time to do it, so let's make it as quick and automated as possible. I ship orders and go on with the rest of my life.

That was how I thought of it, as problem solving. But the other example involving silver is probably a little closer to an emotional reaction, I would say. This was a silver trade. My account had gotten up to—think about this, in the early years of trading—I want to say $50,000 to $100,000. I can't remember the exact number. I hit the same silver upswing that the Hunts were trying to corner—back in those days. I'm doing the silver solely, and I'm the trend follower, I'm going to stick with this, and I've got so many contracts. I let my profits run and was going to cut losses short. And silver's starting to go limit up, down, all over the place and the Hunt stuff comes out, and it collapses back and I've got my stops in. I'm fine, but I saw my account go from like $100,000 up to $500,000 in just a month or six weeks or something insane.

I saw it in the next two weeks go down to $250,000. I ended up making, I don't know, $150,000 on the one trade and at that level it was probably a 150% return on my portfolio. This was way before I understood what I understand now. But out of that I can tell you without a doubt I was watching silver every day. I almost didn't care about the rest of my portfolio. I was very emotionally attached. As it would go up and down and all over the place, I said to myself, "Wait a second …"

Michael: You caught yourself with that emotional attachment.

Tom: I caught myself with the emotional attachment. I always had this sort of tendency in my brain to be able to sit back at the end of the day and observe how I interacted with the day. It's a very useful thing to have an observer self that can be impartial. It sounds like a split personality, but I'm not meaning to make it sound crazy. You just want to be introspective, and you want to be non-judgmental. You want to sit there and say, "How did you do today? Were you even keeled? Did you do all the things you were supposed to do today? Did you get mad at somebody? Did you get overly excited to the point of missing something? Did you get emotional here?" An accounting summary of how the day went.

When I'd looked at the silver thing, I decided I was right in being a good trend follower, putting my stops in, letting the profits run, and cutting the losses short. But there was no reason why I had to let my emotions go up and down and all over the place if I just controlled the size of my position. And that led me to my very first risk control scheme, which was to say that as the stops got further and further away, in the case of silver, my risk was humongous. There was no reason to have five or 10 positions. Maybe all I needed was six, maybe I only needed four, or maybe I only needed one contract.

At TrendStat, when the Gulf War broke out, I think we had maybe one or two clients that ended up with one crude oil contract on after the volatility went from 32 overnight to 40 and back down, then opened up the next day at 22 or something. That was insane volatility and it just completely kicked all of the positions out of everybody's portfolios because nobody had enough equity to afford even one contract.

Michael: Are you a golfer?

Tom: I just came back from the range actually.

Michael: I'm not a huge golf fan, but I follow it enough, and I caught the end of the Masters [2012]. Some of my family's from the South and we loved watching the great southern character Bubba Watson. He hits this shot, basically lays it all out there, and wins the Masters. I take nothing away from him because some of our legendary sports feats are one shot, and you go down in the hall of fame with that. But here you are, you're talking about your process. Tom is focused on process. Process, process, process. You're not sitting around necessarily thinking about the outcome, you're focused on your process. You're grinding it out.

I look at Bubba's shot and see parallels with trading through the financial crisis. I thought about some of the guys that did exceptionally well in the real estate crisis, like John Paulson and Michael Burry. These guys are exceptionally smart and they made some great trades. But maybe you can explain the idea of laying it all on the line. In the world of money, explain trying to hit one home run versus grinding out a career. Maybe lay out the pros and cons to people.

Tom: I think a lot of people have indicated that Buffett falls under this rule, in that he's made the lion's share of his profits off of a select few very big home runs that he has hit over his entire career. But he's had plenty of losers along the way too and that gets glossed over a lot. The winners, of course, have more than paid for the losers, as we find in most trend following cases. That's fine. He has a big image that way.

But examine the TrendStats of the world that are just grinding it out and trying to keep their clients happy and not do anything too flashy. I think I would summarize my image in the industry back in the day as boring. I think a lot of people probably would not have gotten too awfully excited.

Michael: It was never boring to you though, was it?

Tom: It was never boring to me. I was running a nice business. I thought we had a good clientele, and we had a good crew of staff at TrendStat. I enjoyed running the business. I'm enjoying retirement now that I'm not running it. I probably would enjoy life every day no matter what I was doing. But I think the lesson to be learned here is this: If you want to hit the home run, that's fine, but let's not consider that Bubba Watson was not *running his process.*

He likes to move the ball. He was out at my club just a few weeks ago and ended up shooting 67 there from the back tees and made it look easy. Went and shot 56 the next day up at Estancia, which is a pretty difficult desert course. He likes to move the ball, so he can take a shot, he's a leftie, that shot was well in his wheelhouse. He can imagine it, he can hit a wedge, turn it down and he's going to make that ball go left or right a whole lot more than most people probably could humanly do. But that's his normal way of playing. That shot at the Masters wasn't out of his comfort level. That was *his* process.

Michael: I interviewed Paul Mulvaney last summer. Paul had his trend following system and when he came into the fall of 2008 he had no earthly idea that October of '08 would produce him 40% in the month. However, he was following his process. I think that's the exact point you're making, isn't it?

Tom: Yeah, and the same thing's true of currency programs in '97 when the yen-dollar was down to 80 or something. It turned around. I forget whether it came down from 150 or then turned around and went back to 140 or something. It was a huge swing one way, a huge swing the other way. My trade just kept rolling every month, rolling it, rolling it, rolling it. I'm in the same trade for a year and a half. People think of trading as, "You buy today and you sell next week." This was buying and selling over a whole year and a half in currencies, for crying out loud.

But that made me so much money, made the clients so much money. With the incentive fees after that and everything else—it was probably a record year. And I had no clue that was going to happen.

I'm sort of an amateur economist; I understand a lot about economics and if you watch some of my Facebook posts you can see which way I lean on a lot of things.

Michael: You have opinions, Tom? [Laughing]

Tom: Yeah, I have opinions. I am more libertarian by philosophy, but I like to examine economics from the standpoint of the behavior of the people involved with the decision. If you look at decision-making from that standpoint, usually you can figure out which way economics will go.

Michael: I'm now holding in my hands a document: "When to allocate to a CTA—buy them on sale," by Tom Basso, from a few years ago. It's amazing how many times still to this day I will talk to traders that are either running their own accounts or trading a fund, and they have this mentality. And I've got a buddy who runs a small fund who literally will look at some systematic index of trend followers for extra guidance—not part of his system, but he kind of thinks that it actually correlates sometimes when his fund starts to gear up on positions.

Tom: Trend following is driven by the fact that there're asymmetrical returns. There're those big long runs like the Japanese yen trade that I just talked about, where sometimes when I total up all of the TrendStat trades over an entire year, maybe two or three of the trades paid for all the profits. If you could isolate them, pick them up and say, "Okay I could just get these three trades." That was the difference between zero and whatever it was we made that year. All the rest of the trades maybe even netted out to zero. There were some years where it was that close.

If you make the assumption that there're going to be periods of time when the market goes sideways, during that type of environment trend followers are not going to make money, because there's no trend to follow. Typically, depending on where your time frames are, there isn't a trend long enough for the "once a day guy" to really catch much.

On the other hand, there're going to be periods like back in '97 when the Japanese yen goes crazy or maybe in the future when the dollar goes down a lot. Those types of trades more than pay up for all the losses during the sideways periods. If you then make the assumption that there's always an end to a sideways period, there's always an end to the profitable period, then it makes sense to look at a trend follower who's trading lots of markets. Lots of noise, creating drawdowns, lots of trending markets creating profitable periods to rebalance yourself when one trader makes too much money and is getting really leveraged and going crazy. Maybe you back off some money there, and you spread it among other traders that are acting a little more conservative so you might be able to hold onto those profits during the next static sideways period when everybody is going to tend to lose money.

And vice versa, when you get somebody in a deep drawdown—unless he's changed something or you've comply lost trust in what he's doing—then balance right back into the guy that's on the biggest drawdown because he's coming up on the next period, which will be a profitable period again.

It seems like the industry does exactly the opposite though. I wrote another white paper called "Performance Gap," which was the difference between CTA returns and client returns. It turns out for everybody over $75 million that had a five-year track record in the MA database (the Barclays database these days), the time-weighted return the CTA was actually providing by trading was greater than the dollar-weighted return the clients actually got. Clients chase the hot track record and pull out at the bottom, and all that nonsense.

It's very frustrating and sad. It saddened me to see my clientele out there doing stuff that hurt themselves—stopped them from making a good return. I wrote about it though, and it didn't seem to do any good to anybody.

Michael: Psychologically, why would you say that investors don't invest on drawdowns?

Tom: I think psychologically because they don't really understand trading. They can't deal with their own psychology, and they don't realize how important psychology is. What ends up happening is when they see trades down, they start extrapolating that dotted line down, and start calculating that it's going to be X months before it's totally gone or something.

Likewise, I think psychology on the upside is, "This guy's got a great track record for five years, and it keeps going up and up, and it never goes down, so let's draw that dotted line up to off the top of the chart." Which one would I rather have? I'd rather, in my mind, have that guy that's going off the top of the chart rather than the one that's going to lose all my money. They don't step back from themselves and realize the trap they're putting themselves in.

And clients don't understand why trend followers have made money over the long run. I'm sure you get tons of criticism and hocus-pocus. I see some of the Facebook comments and it's really easy to sit there and plot the monthly volatility of a market. I've done it. In TrendStat's case, I don't know how many different markets we did it on, but the months where there was large volatility were the months that were profitable by trend following strategies. Months with small volatility were months where the system basically lost money.

So large volatility profit, low volatility and low direction, are losses. It's as simple as if you looked at a whole year of monthly returns and monthly types of indexes in the various markets being traded. You should almost be able to predict what should have been the average CTA's return for February, because these things occurred—it was probably a losing month because these things occurred; or it was probably a winning month because these things occurred. It was a big winning month or a small winning month. You could actually work it out if you had the data and you understood where trend following returns came from.

But all these fancy people with all their doctorates and all their computers and staff don't seem to be able to figure that out, and so here I was in TrendStat's case buying my own programs when they were in a drawdown. Meanwhile, my clients are calling up and firing me, and then people would be throwing money into my hedge funds when I was making new highs. At new highs, I'm taking some money off the table and giving it away to other managers, or doing other things with it. I'd try to salt it away to take some off the table and even out my portfolio a bit.

I found myself doing exactly the opposite of what my clients were doing all the time. And I'm trying to convince them to do what I'm suggesting they do, but they would not hear anything of it.

Michael: Some folks are just never going to change.

Tom: It is one of the several reasons why I decided to call it a day and move onto golf, fishing, cooking, dancing, and singing.

Michael: Singing? Are you going to sing for us? I was on stage with Ed Seykota and his banjo a couple of years ago. What are you singing for us today?

Tom: Oh, I could.

Michael: What kind of singing?

Tom: Well, I like [he sings] "Fly me to the moon ... and let me live among those stars."

Michael: There we go. I've got a first!

Let's get back to trading and markets. Sometimes when I talk to folks that have been in your position, running a successful fund for a long time, nice track record, they say things that most people from the outside looking in don't expect to hear.

I had a chance to speak with David Harding over in London several times, and he started talking about looking to be a cockroach and looking to be like Madonna. And then Salem Abraham is talking about how to avoid a meteor strike. Clearly, they're talking about surviving. The reality is to have the chance to make it you've got to be there still.

Tom: Exactly. One of the reasons that you're able to be talking to me right now is that by being able to control my risk and volatility, I was able to avoid the meteor strike that Salem would talk about, or David's cockroach thing. Both are interesting analogies. I looked at it as, "I have to play today's game so that I can play the game tomorrow."

If I'm out of the game tomorrow, I've done no good for anybody. You've got to be able to keep playing the game. It's like the casino, in that you're trying to get the statistics on your side, and I think trend following does that well. It does it even better if you use very, very good money management models. Control your risk, control your volatility, control your margin, control the types of markets you select to trade, and that's where a lot of the work is very fruitful.

And I think once you have something you feel comfortable works, and you understand how it works intimately—I mean down into your soul, you know exactly what type of market is going to feed your profits and what type of market is going to leave you licking your wounds—then the statistics are going to end up working out in your favor over the long run. You will be able to keep coming back and playing that game tomorrow. You will be a survivor, and you're going to have a 28- or 30-year run in the industry, like I did. Be around long enough so that people actually recognize your name because you've been at so many MFA conferences or MRA conferences and shaken so many people's hands, and had people interview you, and been quoted in *The Wall Street Journal*. It's just because you survived. It wasn't necessarily because you were flashy.

Michael: I regularly see this, where people really, truly imagine they're going to make money every month. Somehow or another, they're going to make money every month, and I'm sure there's probably somebody out there doing it, maybe because their server's right next to the exchange server or something, they're trading on light speed, something that I don't even understand.

If a track record exists that shows me making 1% to 2% every month with never a down month, I say to myself, "I've either got Long-Term Capital Management on my hands—a strategy that's gonna blow up—or Bernard Madoff on my hands."

Tom: Yeah, I would agree with that. Or a third solution that Eric Crittenden (co-founder of Longboard Capital Management) would say: "You've got a short volatility manager, probably." And short volatility would mean, it'd be something like selling naked options. If you sell them far enough out and you sell them far enough away from the money, the vast majority of the time, the option expires worthless, and you make that money.

So you can produce profits this month, the next month, the next month, and then you have the Long-Term Capital scenario, where somebody's leveraged a whole lot, and that short volatility comes home to roost with a very large movement in the market. Eventually the volatility blows up though, and they're short the volatility. It just kills them. And with the leverage and everything else ... three years of monthly profits just go down the drain. They blow up, and they're gone.

So, yes, I'm very suspicious of track records that are professing to be trend followers and doing month after month of profits. My hat would be off to them. You've got to be really figuring that puzzle out, because it's a tough nut to crack.

Michael: Let me go at Professor Tom again. I'm showing up at your class, and it's Financial Psychology 101. I'm 18 years old, I really don't know much about anything, and I'm forcing you to go back in time to how you would communicate to that audience, because in many ways that audience is the general audience out there. What are you saying on the first day of class when you start the presentation? How are you getting people to come to the point where they're ultimately learning your foundation, your background and your knowledge? What do they have to know in that first week? What are some of the basics that we really want people to get?

Tom: Before you can even deal with simple things—like what a moving average would do, or what a trend following model might be, or how to control risk or volatility—you'd have to actually know how to put in a stock trade. My mom, for instance, the 83-year-old retiree, would not even know what a stockbroker was—wouldn't have one, doesn't know how to even articulate an order, so she would have a hard time even doing the basic first trade.

You'd have to teach people something basic about the market, how to put a trade in and know that the market is a place where buyers and sellers come together. Once you get past the nuances of whether it's futures markets and you're dealing with ticks, or currency markets and you're dealing with pips, and so on and so forth, then maybe in the first day you could get on to the three pillars of success for trading. One of them is understanding what it is that you're trying to do.

What I mean by that is each person's going to have to come to some conclusion on why the markets do what they do. There're maybe those that think economics drives it, because they're economics majors and that's what they want to base their decision on. If you come to that conclusion, you're going to have to build risk, volatility and portfolio selection around what your comfort level is, and then you're going to have to work out a buy and sell decision model. Once you have those three things together, you have a shot at being successful even if you're an economist.

It wouldn't be my cup of tea, but I'm sure there're economists out there that are doing just fine if they can get everything together. But that's the way I would approach it. I would try to teach those three things. The understanding of what you want to do and what makes the markets work from your viewpoint. It's basically what drives the individual doing the trade, because it's you who has to decide to stick with the system, or abandon it or add new markets, or tweak the strategy, or all the things that go on. And if you're not comfortable with that, it isn't going to happen. But you must also have control of what markets you trade. Some are going to make sense to you, and some are not. You're also going to need a decision model that could be something like a breakout on a chart, or a moving average going over. You're going to need something to trigger your action, and I think those three things, you get those together, you've probably got a shot at least at getting into the game.

Michael: I want to know what Tom is thinking about these days, besides the fun part—the singing, the golf, the dancing. I know your brain is still thinking about stuff. What's the big picture?

Tom: I would say the thing that I think about the most, and I've noticed several Facebook posts by some of the friends that you and I have in common, is there're a lot of us out here in the trading world. I've traded 80 commodity markets, 30 currency markets, all sorts of ETFs and mutual funds, and I used to trade stocks, I used to trade options, I used to trade Treasury bonds even, and I sit here watching us running up another $5 trillion in debt. We're debasing the dollar with all the quantitative easing.

And I'm sitting here trying to figure out each day how I am supposed to financially survive in retirement and protect and grow my assets. I'm a guy that has traded almost everything that is tradable. I feel really sorry for the people like my mother, who is confused by a CD, because even I am having a hard time coming up with ways to make sense of it. The trend followers are absolutely going to nail it; but when they win the race, they're going to look around and say "Yeah, but …"

Michael: Post-apocalyptic.

Tom: Yeah. I sit there and I think, "Okay, let's see. If you're a successful trader, and you're part of the 1%, and you're looking at what it is you're supposed to be doing, to position your portfolio so that you or your client can preserve purchasing power over the long run, you've got to increase your net worth to keep your net wealth the same in an era where the dollar's getting debased. It's very difficult to see how to do that.

Michael: You've seen many different climates, many different markets, and many different socio-economic political patterns. Are you expressing a feeling about 2012 and going forward that's much different than you felt in your lifetime?

Tom: I feel like we're setting up the potential for some very large moves which trend followers are going to love.

I'm not making predictions. I just have the sense that we're straining the financial structure of the United States to the point where now debt is more than 100%, it's like 108% GDP. That's getting to be pretty unusual and rarefied air. In other words, if you look at the economic statistics of the United States and even the rest of the world, we're pushing to levels that have not been seen before. When you get that type of stuff you have the potential for collapses, you have the potential for bubbles, and the bubbles bursting possibly. You have some very high volatility potential.

I have no predictions about which way anything is going to go. I hope that trend following will probably be there to capitalize on a lot of those major moves. However, at the same time as I'm capitalizing on it, I'm concerned that the value of what you have when you're all done with it, while greater net worth than you have today, might not be worth as much to go out and buy anything with.

Looking at things from a retirement situation, my grandfather lived to 98, and I'm 59 now. I'm in great health, I'm enjoying life, but if I were to live to my grandfather's age of 98, I've still got 39 years to go. That's longer than I was in the business. It's pretty interesting to think in those terms, decades. I've got to manage my portfolio and figure out how to at least keep my net wealth roughly the same, so I can continue to enjoy a nice retirement.

That's the one thing that crosses my mind more and more lately, and it's a tough puzzle. The solution is out there in the hands of the entire country, not just me. I can't control what happens around me. I've traveled all over the world, and I've thought about, "Now, what if I moved to Australia? How would that be? Or Switzerland, or Britain?" I've been to all those places and they're all fine in their own ways, nice places to visit, but I call the USA home and I like Phoenix, Arizona. I think it's a great place to live. You'd have to be hard pressed to get me out of here. But given that I've made that decision to stay here, and I've got the state of Arizona, and the country of the United States around me, I have to live with hundreds of thousands of pages of tax code to deal with my taxes, and I have to deal with all the different economic decisions that are made that I'm pulling out my hair over and saying, "Yeah, you've got to be kidding me. That's a stupid thing to do."

But if we keep making those stupid decisions, I feel like I'm going to be in the middle of this chaotic nonsense trying to survive along with everybody else—admittedly with maybe more knowledge about what I might be able to do. But at this moment, it's really hard for me to figure out an easy answer to be able to articulate to someone and say, "I think we should do the following, one, two, three, four, five, and that'll probably set you up to be able to survive fine." I don't think it's just as easy as going out and buying gold coins, for instance—which you see the ads for all the time on the television. I think gold is fine—it might go up, it might go down. People may take your coin in terms of buying something, or they may not want your coin.

There's a lot of unknown out there. I think back to the '70s, '80s, and the economy was a little bit going sideways. It wasn't really robustly growing. After Reaganomics kicked in, it kind of got good for a while, then through the Clinton years we sort of did all right. In the Bush years we did okay. But we've strained the system so much now that I wonder whether there aren't some really big moves coming up. So I would encourage everybody to be a trend follower here, but good luck figuring out how to deal with it.

Michael: I'd like to ask you about entrepreneurship. How is being an entrepreneur? Do you ever think about how different that makes you in terms of your thinking, your feeling?

Tom: All the time. I guess not so much now, except as I observe people who aren't. Van K. Tharp has some programs for traders on the psychology of things, and I did some speaking with him for some time. Somewhere along the way I decided that the easiest way for me to deal with my entire life and the universe around me was to take responsibility, personally, for everything that happened in my life, even if it was caused by somebody else. To figure out how I could work my judgment to the point where I could be responsible.

If you are responsible for everything, and then you jump to the next line of thinking that you can then take some control of it, and change decisions or change your path or do something different, you can move your whole life far afield. I mean, I started as a chemical engineer and I ended up as a currency trader by the time I retired. The immediate question everybody asks is, "How the heck did that happen?"

It happened one day at a time. When I was at Monsanto as a chemical engineer, every four years there were booms and busts, and the chemical engineers would be hired one year and then four years later were getting laid off. I wanted to have a backup, so I needed to trade my portfolio, build up my net worth so I had a backup. If I did get laid off, I could control my own destiny and live a year or two while looking for another chemical engineering position in tough times.

One thing leads to another and pretty soon you're trading so much money, people notice it, and they want you to manage some of their money. You get sucked into the money management business, but you still take responsibility for making that decision to say, "Okay, I don't want chemical engineering anymore, I'm going to go be a money manager." That's all within your control if you're taking responsibility for everything in your life. And I think that's what entrepreneurs tend to do. Entrepreneurs tend to take control, and they realize that they're making it happen. They're not going to wait for somebody to hand it to them.

Michael: My father was always fond of saying that he just didn't want to have a gig where he had to say, "Yes, sir," to an A-hole all day long.

Tom: But even in the money management business we've got clients. I mean, there's always somebody to answer to. We'd have money laundering audits when we were in the currency trading business where the IRS would come in and look at us. There's always somebody …

Michael: You've got to say, "Yes, sir," to them. Otherwise you're in trouble.

Tom: They'll stay for another week just because. They'll make your life miserable.

Q&A with Mr. Serenity

EPISODE 83: NOVEMBER 28, 2012

Michael: I have a quick opening question that I want to throw at you, Tom. I know you saw the video of the philosopher Alan Watts that I posted on my site. Alan Watts asked the question, "If money was no object, what would you do? How would you manifest your desires? How would you unfold your life?" How would you respond to that?

Tom: I came upon my personal answer to this sometime in my 20s. Someone could ask, "What if you had more money, what would that get you?" And you try to answer the question. And then they say, "Okay, what if you got that?" Well, then I would be able to do this. You can keep hammering at this forever saying, "Okay, so now let's give you that, and what do you have now?"

What it comes down to is happiness. You can make a choice no matter what your lot in life. How many poor people have a smile on their face, and enjoy every day? How many wealthy people are miserable? It's really a choice that each person has to make to just be happy.

I think money provides a lot of flexibility. It probably provides a little better chance at having proper nutrition, or better ability to exercise and keep your body healthy. There're all those little things. But in the end, money can provide happiness as long as you allow it to.

Michael: I thought it was important for you to put that out there at the beginning, before we get into the rest of the Q&A. I think it's important that maybe people can see what's important at the very top.

25

Tom: You want to be a good trend follower, and you become a master at it. So 20, 30 years go by, and you're doing very well, and you're managing your own money, and you can still make your life miserable. You can take some of the money and go buy some real estate and complicate your life. Or you can have five divorces and further complicate it. Or you could have all sorts of other extraneous things that you allow to intrude on your happiness.

Just being a good trend follower doesn't somehow make you happy. You can choose to be happy before you become a trend follower and you can choose to be happy after you're a successful trend follower.

Michael: Now that that's explained, let's jump into some of these questions.

This first question is from Dan Montag and it says, "Tom, how do you, Mr. Serenity, manage your emotions during a loser? Any changes today since the book, *The New Market Wizards*?"

Tom: That's a good question; Dan is a smart guy. I have a concept in my mind that I labelled "anchored to the wind." When I'm on a super-fast winning streak and money is flowing in, almost in record amounts and I almost can't believe it, I keep trying to force my mind into a place where I remember back to the struggle for four years to get my commodity account to even break-even. Or I think about my latest drawdown and how I felt during that drawdown. What I try to do mentally is bring my enthusiasm back to neutral.

And so the opposite is also true for Dan's question. I try in losing periods to go back and remember those times when I had every market on the page turn green and I was making money hand over fist. I try to balance out my frustration, anxiety—anything negative that I am feeling during a drawdown. You're trying to remember back to those times when you had everything on your page green and everything making a lot of money, and it sort of brings you back to neutral again the other way.

The goal is to try to go into each day dead neutral and try to end each day about the same. It's just another piece of data in a long, long stream of thousands of days of trading over a lifetime that are all just data points. When you step back and look at it from that distance, it sort of calms you. It calms you on the upside, it calms you on the downside, and it allows you to just think rationally.

Michael: The next question: "Tom, you conclude most of your Facebook posts with the expression, 'Enjoy the ride.' What drove you to that conclusion, and was there a period in your life where it was a challenge to enjoy the ride?"

Tom: I usually put "enjoy the ride" to remind all those traders out there that there's no final destination to all of this, and we all eventually are going to pass away. We're not going to be trend followers anymore, we're going to be dead. I think you need to take every day, and see the magical things that happen around you, and be open to new ideas, open to observations about the world that exists out there, and that's what it's all about.

Trying to get to some final destination and putting yourself through hell to get there when the destination may not be quite what you think it is, or might be a little bit disappointing when reality sets in, is a waste of time. You don't want to get there and say, "Well, is this all there is?" Enjoying the ride is everything to me. I start each day with, "I can't wait to attack it." This morning I was hitting golf balls, playing with a new concept for about two hours and ten minutes or so.

I was just enjoying a beautiful Scottsdale morning and I was the only one on the range. It was very quiet, and it was beautiful. That's what enjoying the ride is all about. It's not just about trading your brains out.

Michael: Before we started today I did a yoga session with a teacher, and it was about an hour and a half to two hours long. At the very end, as I'm lying on my back, eyes closed, she read a passage that was almost verbatim what you just said. The moment of now, enjoy the journey. It will all be over at some point in time, so try not to live in the future, don't live in the past—you've got right now.

Tom: Exactly.

Michael: "Was there a period in your life where there was a challenge to enjoying the ride that really stands out?"

Tom: Yes. That was before I understood a lot about myself—probably in my 20s when I was working as a chemical engineer. I was trying to get an MBA. I was designing a custom home that I was about to build four years later up in the woods, southwest of St. Louis. I was starting up Kennedy Capital, which is a stock manager investment advisory firm in St. Louis, and I was also trading commodities. That pretty much consisted of waking up in the morning, going hard all day, then falling asleep exhausted, and getting up in the morning, and doing it all again.

Weekends, when I wasn't working as a Monsanto engineer, I would spend my time doing research on my commodity account and trying to improve what I was doing in stock trading.

And I think at this stage of life, from an energy level and at my age of 60 and all, I think I pace myself a whole lot better. I do take on a lot of things and sometimes find myself rushing a little bit, but there's always that time in the day where I say, "Okay, time to put it away and go do something fun." I always try to get a little bit of enjoying the ride into every day if I can.

Michael: Larry says, "Can you ask Tom about his exit strategies on winning positions? A lot of traders know to use stops for losers, but exiting winners can be a bit trickier."

Tom: Okay, I know Larry, and he is a smart trader himself. I listened to his podcast and loved it. The answer to Larry's question is pretty simple. I don't see a whole lot of difference between a winning trade and a losing trade. I think of it in these terms: If the direction is up today, I want to be long, and I want to put a stop sell behind that position. As long as the direction continues to be up, I'm either keeping the stop where it was or moving it in the direction of up. So I'm moving it up behind the position.

When the direction shifts and goes the other way, the stop eventually gets hit and the down direction is now in place, and I wouldn't want to be in the position anymore. I try to simplify it down to something that simple. I don't try to second guess and say, "Okay, well, I had 20%, and therefore I should do something different in terms of trying to take the profit or whatever." I just let it run.

I remember a very famous question to Ed Seykota. I was listening to a talk he was giving, probably when I was in my 30s. The person asked, "Ed, what's your objective when you get into a trade?" And Ed looked at him and said, "Pretty much the moon. When I get into the trade, I'm hoping this thing goes long, and I'm going to be in it for the rest of my life, and

I never have to do another trade." I mean, that's a good answer. There's no reason to think it couldn't; reality would say that I've never had that happen yet, but let them run.

Michael: And have a plan if it doesn't run.

Tom: If it doesn't run, it's going to change direction and hit the stop, with a loss. If it runs and then falters and changes direction, you're going to hit the stop and have a profit. But it's the same exact trade as far as I'm concerned. I don't try to differentiate it. I know some people do, and I don't see any reason why you couldn't look at that as a research project, but it just never made any sense to me psychologically. If the direction's down, I don't want to be in it; I don't care whether they have a profit or a loss, I just don't want to be in it.

Michael: Clint Stevens and Steve Burns both have a question on hedges. They would like to hear your thoughts on the edge you have and your trading method by using hedges to decrease losses in down trends instead of exiting your long positions.

Tom: It takes a little time but it's pretty simple. Say you take any kind of strategy you want, whether it be purely technical or partially fundamental. I like to screen stocks and ETFs based on a little bit of fundamentals. If I'm looking for high dividend yield, that would be a factor you could screen positions on, for instance. Valuations like PE ratios and things like that. I'd rather buy something a little bit cheaper than buy something extremely pricey.

That being said, let's say I'm smart enough to put together a diversified portfolio of longs. Let's say I did that last September, just for the sake of argument here. I just happened to look as I was closing down my market stuff just before you called and my equity in my stock portfolio, which has been hedged quite a lot over the last few months, is exactly the same as it was in mid-September. It hasn't gone up or down a nickel.

I've put hedges on every time a down direction occurs, and I've taken them off every time an up direction occurs. Time is clicking by on all those wonderful positions I've put in place, so I'm getting closer to long-term capital gains which I can use for charitable contributions, or I can get a better tax rate on.

Meanwhile, on my hedges I'm short selling the SPY ETF, which is very, very liquid. I can short any time I wish; I can take off any time I wish. It trades sometimes like 30 times a second. What you're doing is buffering your portfolio with the SPY at the same time that your long positions have the ability, over the long run, to become a long-term capital gain and to allow their alpha, if you've done your job right. You're picking them to sort of go through every up and down and show that they can do something for you.

That's where the edge comes in. You've got a long-term gain on your taxes there against the short-term nature of the hedges.

Michael: This is from Brandon Brockman. He says, "Tom, during the strategy development and testing process, what metrics gave you confidence in your system, and what process did you follow in taking a developed system from testing to live trading?"

Tom: This is a good question, but it's not a short answer! It requires a little bit of history and walking through the process. When we came up with a concept at TrendStat, in trying to figure out whether it added value or not, there were a number of different things we did.

First of all, we had a database of cleaned up data that we went through and painstakingly made sure there were no anomalies. Like, for instance, a close or an open that was outside the high-low range. That is an obvious one that we used to find in databases all the time, and that can't happen. If we've got an open and a close, it's got to be within the high-low range, or something's wrong.

We cleaned up data and then we would go through and take the concept and program the actual indicator that says buy here, sell there, or do whatever the indicator's trying to do. Then we would try to have some metrics. We primarily looked at largest drawdown, average drawdown, time to recoveries, and we looked a lot at return-to-risk ratios. We'd measure risk by return-to-drawdown; we'd measure return-to-volatility on the returns. Those types of things.

And all of that is great. But I can tell you that in reality, the thing that helped me feel most comfortable with any kind of new indicator was when I'd go into my office, and tell my secretary Lisa, "I'm shutting the door, and I'm going to be going down this research result, and unless it's an emergency, don't bother me." I would take a ruler and I would start with page one, put the ruler on there, and I would read what the market did that day and I would read what the results from the strategy were that day. And I would ask myself this one question: "Did that strategy perform that day like you would have expected it, given the type of market that you had that day?" It's very important to understand it to that level because in the end, that's what causes trend followers, or any traders for that matter, to let go of their system and abandon it when it's having a rough two weeks, or a month, or six months, or a year.

One of the questions was, "What do you do when your strategy's not working?" If you looked at the data of the last couple of months of the market, let's say, and you said, "Based on the strategy and the way I set my strategy up, I would have expected my strategy to have a difficult period in the last couple of months," then that's fine. It it's not broken, don't fix it. Just let it keep going. Wait for the good times. Good times are somewhere in the future probably.

I think a lot of people look at a drawdown as: It's not working anymore. None of my strategies, including when I had all of them together and add them together, ever got to the point where I never had a losing day. They're always going to have losing days. So when I looked at it, I said, "Gee, if I'm having a choppy sideways market, and I've got a trend following model that's getting chopped up a little bit on the sideways market, well that's what I would expect. Let's wait until the next trending market, and I'll be fine."

I got to that level of knowledge by going through day after day after day. I would sit there with six pieces of computer paper, and take a ruler going down the page, looking at every day's data. It would take me hours. But when I got to that level I thought, "I understand it, it's working; I understand exactly how it's going to react to a lot of different things, and the metrics look okay. Let's go turn it on, and put some real money with it."

Michael: Let me throw in a follow-up from Jim Byers: "Can you describe what you learned from your earliest large drawdown?"

Tom: Yeah. That is an easy one to remember. It was a silver trade. I think it was documented in the *Market Wizards* interview. I was merrily going along my way. I think my futures portfolio was about a couple of hundred thousand or something like that. I got into a couple of different silver contracts. This was the time when the Hunts were trying to corner silver. Silver went through the roof. It exceeded any expectation I would ever have. Being the good trend follower I was at that point, I was going to hold on for dear life and just go up and down. Whichever way the market went, I was just going to keep moving my stops as the stops could be justified.

My stops got pretty far away because the market was going so fast upward. At one point I noticed that I had gotten to something like $600,000 or $500,000, something ridiculous. I had made 400% or 500%. I'm still hanging onto the same exact positions. That's when the major drawdown occurred. I got out of the position and my portfolio ended up probably about a quarter of a million or $300,000. I had lost $300,000 just in a matter of weeks when they broke apart the corner and increased the margins. The whole thing just fell apart and went limit down day after day after day.

What I learned from that was that volatility as a percent of the equity in my portfolio need not change. What I mean by that is I had several different silver contracts. There was no reason why I couldn't stay with that silver trade and be a good trend follower and ride it to the bitter end. But I didn't need to hold the same number of contracts at the end as I had when I started out. I could peel off contracts as it went, so that it reduced the volatility to the portfolio but still gave me a significant silver position.

That way, the portfolio acts more like a portfolio instead of 15 things in a silver position where the silver position drives the whole portfolio up or down every day, and the rest of them don't make a difference at all. By volatility adjusting my positions on an ongoing basis, we could take 80 different commodity markets traded by multiple different systems, and the computers could just tell us where the volatility of every single position should be. That way, the portfolio was acting like a portfolio, and no one market could really dominate too much of what was going on that day.

That's what I learned from it. It was a very valuable lesson that sort of expanded into risk controls as a percent of equity. By the end of TrendStat we had lots of different ways of trying to control position size. The bottom line of the position sizing is that every position has a meaningful impact on the portfolio—not a small amount, not a large amount, a meaningful amount. And when you get to that level, then you're truly managing a portfolio.

Michael: There are lots of questions about your use of money management, the types of money management, how you approach risk control and whether you pyramid at all.

Tom: I have viewed money management as an easy calculation. Take the risk to your stop loss of where you are at any point in time, multiply it by the number of contracts—that's your dollars of risk, your net position. Then divide it by the equity in your portfolio, and that's the percent of your portfolio that's at risk at that point due to that one position. You could do the same thing with volatility: You take your volatility of any one position times the number of contracts. Volatility for me was the average true range over the last 20 days. Divide it by the equity, you get a margin, or a volatility as a percent of equity. Margin, you can do the same thing: How much margin for a position times the number of contracts, divided by the equity, you get margin per equity.

You can set fixed levels for every one of those three things. By doing so, you can do a calculation where the computer says, "If I exceed the limits on any of these, I'm going to sell off enough positions to get me back underneath all of those limits." And I even went to the point where I had initial position limits, and I had ongoing existing position limits because when a position becomes profitable and starts running, it's by its very nature going to take on a little extra volatility, a little extra risk. But by now you've got a winning position and it's going your way. You want to let it run.

We came up with a level for initial position risk and initial volatility risk as a percent of equity and sized our portfolios. Then as the markets would run our way, we would allow in a little more room. As it got above those levels, we would start stripping off contracts until we got back to the point where it was within the limits. And yet we would always let our positions run, as Ed Seykota would say, "To the moon."

Michael: Ross Hendricks and Matthew Fry both have questions about system testing. "What kind of advice could you give to the programmer looking to back test for the first time?" And Matthew asks, "Do you believe in walking a system forward? If not, what metrics are best used to monitor the health of your edge, and how do you know when you might make a change?" Ross is really asking, "How do I get started as a beginner in programming my system?" and Matthew's saying, "I want some comment on walking a system forward—how do you know when a change might be needed?"

Tom: Good questions all. Starting out, I had the good fortune in my case to be a chemical engineer, so I took four trend programming and basic programming classes and understood what a program was all about. I was not born with the knowledge of programming, and I don't think anyone is. These are learned skills.

You can buy books on it; you can take classes on it. I would recommend when you're starting out, take a good look at something as simple as an Excel spreadsheet. For a lot of things that I do these days, since I don't have full-time programming staff, I just do my testing in Excel. It's gotten so powerful and so capable. With the gigabytes of hard drive that we have on our computers and with the high processing speeds we have, you can do an awful lot of stuff in Excel today that I could not even program back on my IBM PC in the old days, or on my TRS-80 back in 1980.

Computers are pretty powerful on a small basis, so consider Excel, maybe start there. You can see what's going on a little easier. If you want to try to get a little fancy inside of Excel, you can install visual basic of modules. There're lots of courses and books available on that, too. That's probably where I'd start.

A lot of the canned strategy programs can give you some tools to look at, but my worry is that a lot of those tend to not be geared to exactly the way you're going to end up trading. So it's not giving you a realistic view of what it is you're about to embark on. What I mean by that is sometimes these canned programs don't have the same position sizing that you're going to have, so they might be based on one contract, and the one contract is always one contract. You get the results of one contract, but you don't get the effect of money management in there.

You end up getting a weird look at history. You might become tainted, good or bad, by that. When you're looking at history, you want to become comfortable with your strategy versus various types of markets. You do not want to get to the point where you fall in love with some strategy based on a simulation that was not even done in a rigorous fashion, and then all of a sudden it's falling apart in the future, and you don't have that comfort level that you need to stick it out.

That's how I would start out.

"Walking forward" to me is a term that describes taking a section of time, running a strategy, and then coming out with the results of that strategy, and using that particular database to re-optimize your parameters. Then you're going to go attack the next part of the database, and see what its results are, then use that second section of data so it optimizes the parameters. You then walk that forward to the third chunk of data and so on.

I thought that seemed a bit clunky because that's not the way the real world works. To me, every day was another day. Take true range for example. The average true range over 20 days changes every day. If you have average true range as one of your parameters, it's walking forward every day, and day after day you're going to get a new 20-day period, a new average true range, and things are changing each day.

So you're walking it forward based on that. That's closer to what you actually do in trading every day. I like that type of strategy better than blocking off large sections of data and optimizing that section and then using it on the next chunk of data.

If you want to think of it as walking forward every day, you can certainly do that with your historical databases by calculating the average true range of every 20-day period. Then you start going through the database, make your decisions, make your money management calls, and let the databases keep track of it all. And you're in good shape.

Michael: I've got a question here from Andrew Derbyshire. He's asking how you have handled skepticism toward trend following in the past. For example, thinking about how David Harding was having to handle that on CNBC.

Tom: We certainly had our skeptics and they still exist out there. That's one of the reasons why trend following still works so well. If everybody believed in it, it probably wouldn't work so well.

In the later stages of my career I did some studies that looked at where trend followers make money and where they lose it. I came up with a concept of taking the monthly returns on an assorted portfolio of 20 or 30 different commodities and measured the amount of absolute change in direction in any one market. Then I put that against the profits that CTAs got during those periods. I did this first with our own TrendStat portfolios because I had the detail of market by market by market. I did it later on a macro basis by saying, "What were the average prices of a whole portfolio of things high or low, and what were the profits from the CTA industry, high or low?"

And we found a definite correlation between when markets move and when CTAs make money, or trend followers make money. That should be very logical. I don't see why anybody could disagree with it. I don't see why anybody would think that wouldn't work.

Then the question becomes, "Are you going to have market movement or a market that's just going to sit in one place for the next 20 years?" If you knew that markets were not going to go anywhere for 20 years, I don't think you'd probably want to be a trend follower. You probably don't want to be a trader. You can't make much money if the market isn't going to move, because you've got to buy at one price and sell at a higher price, or sell at a higher price and buy at a lower price. If the market doesn't move at all, you're not going to get a higher or a lower price; you're going to get the same price.

It seems to me markets have to move. It seems to me also, over my lifetime thanks to computers and lots more participation in the markets and so on, all the forces that come together, there's been more volatility rather than less. So there's more potential for things to explode to ridiculously high levels. You've now got the currency being somewhat devaluated with all this QE nonsense that I'm dead against.

If the dollar keeps getting more and more worthless, and things like crude oil are based on the dollar, then people in the Middle East or wherever are going to want more dollars for the same amount of their oil that they're selling us. It seems to me we're going to end up paying it sooner or later. Therefore, you've got this bias for things to go outside of the range where they've been before just because the currency that it's based on is going outside of where it's been before as well.

Given all that, it seems to me that's where trend followers like David Harding are going to over time continue to make money. CNBC and some of the people on the interview shows will never get it because they're looking at the last five minutes of what the Dow did.

That's where the disconnect comes. The edge for trend followers will be in future volatility. There will be more volatility in the future than less and there're going to be a lot more big moves in the future than less. You have to put up with the nonsense in between.

Michael: I remember being invited to CNBC to speak with producers to have me pitch them a show on the spot. I remember walking through that studio and it was so interesting because there was this big bullpen area of all these reporters—the people that you see on TV. And then off to the side is the set.

As a viewer you're sitting there and you see this nice little TV window of what's going on, but when you're inside the studio, and you look at it, you realize, "Wow, this is all very engineered. This is all very fake. This isn't real." And if you stand there and you see it in live, in living color, it's much different than flipping on the TV and seeing what they want you to see within the confines of the borders of your screen.

Tom: And a lot of it's just geared to talking about noise. Why would anybody tuning in want to hear something from David Harding on a strategy that would require a tremendous amount of work to put together, covering the next decade or something, instead of, "I want to know why the Dow's down 50 points today."

Michael: Right.

Tom: That's what the average Joe doesn't get. I wouldn't think CNBC is a place where professional traders go for ideas, except maybe to do the opposite.

Michael: I guess if they see an interview with David Harding and they've never heard *those* types of answers or that type of thought process, maybe some might say to themselves, "I better find out who this guy is and what he does, and maybe I can learn something."

Tom: That would require you having enough knowledge to separate the good pieces of information from David from the bad pieces of information, which would be the announcers that are asking the questions.

Michael: Touché.

Tom: And if you knew that, you probably didn't need to go talk to David Harding.

Michael: Exactly. It's a catch-22. I have a question here from Clint Stevens, who says, "In Jack Schwager's book, *The New Market Wizards*, it suggests that you were not included in the book on a return basis alone, but for this combination of 'serenity,' plus returns." Clint wants to know the development of your trading approach and how you run your life from the ground up. Was the notion of serenity and not being a crazed, overweight, overworked trader sitting there nonstop with no life always in the plan?

Tom: Yes, it was to a large extent. It's slightly different than you would expect though in that my view of my job as a money manager was to manage client assets—it wasn't to manage my assets. When I listen to clients, and ask them what they like and don't like, I learn as a money manager that really the average client out there sadly does not allow their money manager they've hired to do what that money manager is capable of.

If a manager trades as he wants to trade, and the portfolio goes up and down too much, it makes the clients nervous and they fire you. Clients always want to chase after the returns and give you the money when it's high on your equity curve. And when your equity curve's gone through a drawdown, they want to pull it out. This is very self-defeating from the standpoint of performance fees. It's also very self-defeating from the standpoint of clients making actual returns on investments. I determined very early on in the process that it was my job to try to make the clients as good a client as I could, so they would allow me to be the best money manager I could be.

When you do that, you start designing your strategies around the client, not around you. Now, because clients had a lot less risk tolerance than I did, it indirectly fed into my quality of life because I created strategies that were a lot tamer, that had a lot less variation. I attempted to try to stick to return-to-risk ratios that were good and sort of boring. Jack Schwager kept having people say, "You should really interview Tom; he's a very interesting guy." And Jack, being the caffeinated New Yorker at the time, working for Prudential-based futures and director of research, I believe, he's looking for the sizzle that'll sell the *Market Wizards* books. He was trying to find these guys that have created quadruple, hundreds, thousands of percent returns and are legends on the street. That sells books and my story isn't that compelling. It's an engineer that turns into a money manager who's got some kind of tame returns and just cruises along.

On the surface, Jack didn't see much there of interest. But when people kept telling him over and over again that he needed to interview me, he kept getting puzzled and thinking, "What the heck does everybody think is so interesting about Tom?" And when he got done interviewing me and found out how I designed everything to have a life, and that I had a really fun life, he realized sort of wistfully, I think, that he hadn't figured out how to do that for himself yet.

He indicated to me that out of the two books he wrote on the *Market Wizards* up to that point, my style of trading probably in the end would be something he would be most interested in following versus all the others, because it led to a peacefulness and a control of the trading process to the point where there wasn't a lot of angst. I think Jack originally came to trading thinking there has to be stress, it's a macho type of endeavor, and you've got to go through big returns. You've got to suck it up, and ride the equity curve. It was all nonsense, really. It was just his own biases that led to that thinking, and I kind of opened up his eyes to another world.

Michael: I think it's the lifestyle choice that I saw my father make. My father is a dentist, and he decided even in his 20s before he had any practice to speak of, before he had any real grand revenue coming in the door or anything, that he was going to work a four-day work week, and he's taken off Friday every week. He built that into his system as a young man. There are ways, techniques and ideas we can use to think about doing things differently.

To get back to the Alan Watts video we discussed at the very beginning— he was bringing a lot of Eastern thoughts to the Western world. He asks the question, "How can you structure your life differently, and think about it early on?" How do you avoid getting stuck on the treadmill?

Tom: Exactly. I'm in retirement. TrendStat's no longer there; I don't have a staff of ten; I don't have 40 computers. I have one PC that I pretty much do most of my work on, and we're talking on another PC right now. I have to think to myself, "All right; let's see." I don't have the staff, I don't have the backups, but I need to create good trading strategies. So I morphed them to a different style of trading in different markets that I trade now. I never traded orange juice at TrendStat because we were too big, but now I can trade orange juice, so I trade orange juice. You adjust with the conditions that exist at the time.

In addition to my trading different markets, what else do I do in retirement? I want to be able to go hit some golf balls today for two hours plus. I don't want to be tied to sitting here in front of the computer all day and looking at charts and ruining my eyes. I'd rather go out and prune trees in the backyard, plant some flowers, go work out, go for a hike, go play golf, and all these other things that I like to do.

So if I'm going to create a trading strategy, why don't I design something that works for my lifestyle so that my lifestyle's exactly what I want it to be, and yet I can still apply good trading strategy principles to my trading? I think that's simple to do if you just start from the question, "How do I want my trading strategy to operate with my lifestyle?"

I've often said, "If you're a traveling salesman, you're on the road five days a week, and you're home on weekends, why not do a Saturday morning trading style?" You can take once a week data, you look at it Saturday morning, you make your decisions, you send them in electronically, and then you go on the road Sunday night again.

Michael: It's actually been surprising me in the last couple of years to learn how many large funds, large trend following funds, use weekly bar systems.

Tom: Absolutely. It gives you a different angle. One of the reasons some of the large CTAs are struggling is the dollars they're managing are so huge. They affect the market when they go in and out, so they have to start getting in or out over two or three days and going to weekly charts. As long as you do the rest of the work on risk control and portfolio diversification, there's no reason to think you can't be successful. It might change your return stream or your return-to-risk profile a little bit, but that's what these big guys have to do. They cannot afford to make any trade that is not an essential trade because they've got too much money.

It's hard as a CTA when you've got a lot of different forces trying to shove money at you, your employees are trying to make a career of being in the business, and you're trying to go into new markets. It's hard to turn down money coming in. You really need your own personal levels, and say, "No, this is going to be $100 million, and we're going to shut it down at $100 million. If it gets above $100 million, we're going to start sending money back to you all."

A lot of CTAs have done that. It gives an indication that you're choking on the amount of money that you're managing. The allocators that are giving you the money are starting to think, "Gee, this guy's sending money back, that means he's really struggling to keep the money invested." Or, maybe they say, "He's being true to us and not diluting our returns by trading once a week," or something.

There are two sides to the story, but it's something that puts a spotlight on that trader. He has to be able to withstand the scrutiny and explain why he's sending money back. But some people just don't send the money back and then their returns get diluted over time.

Michael: One of the things that I've done in my books is show the validity of a trading strategy by looking at different traders that have historical track records and say, "Look at how this has performed over many, many decades."

When you start to talk about the money under management and assets, sometimes the money management gets blended into the two of them. Your life today is one man, no staff, and a nice life. For example, take John W. Henry recently closing down his shop. For me it's hard to criticize a man who was in this space for 30 years and was very successful.

Tom: He survived.

Michael: Yeah. He survived. He had huge assets under management and then he decides he wants to go into another business, completely unrelated, makes a fortune in that. Is it surprising necessarily that he doesn't have every ball in the world bouncing up in multiple Fortune 500 businesses? Sometimes you need to step back a little for perspective on this kind of thing.

Tom: Yeah you do; you really do. John Henry is a good example. He ran a little bit more leverage than I would have run, so he had a little bit more up and down, but he was able to continue to attract attention and had enough marketing capability or sales capability that he was able to keep the business running for a long, long time. Hats off to him for doing it. In the end everybody should consider, "What does John Henry want to do with his day? Does he want to manage a futures trading firm that he doesn't have a whole lot of interest in?" It's just a big liability and he's got a very deep pocket. Why put yourself through that liability?

Michael: Yeah, and if people think about it, it's not necessarily surprising. Just like you've made this transition. I knew this years ago the moment John bought the team. You say, "Well he's obviously interested in other stuff too, and it's hard to be interested in two very big things like that in one lifetime."

Tom: Who knows, he may be looking at something else completely different that we don't even know about.

Michael: You have to salute that. The moment of now and you adjust to the situation. It's a fantastic story. Look, you and I both know that there's a lot of armchair quarterbacks that sit out there on the sidelines drinking a Budweiser, 50 lbs. overweight, watching the football game, throwing out criticism. But you've got to give props to the guy who's in the game, and he's sweating away and making it happen. I have to salute that 100%.

Tom: Sure.

Michael: You've got a coin flip entry method experiment that you've done and Larry wanted you to reiterate that. It focuses people less on entries, which is the favorite thing for most traders when they're getting started. It puts more emphasis on the exit and proper money management.

Tom: Right. Usually when novice traders start out, the biggest thing is to read a book on trading. They read *Trend Following Manifesto* or something. They find out a lot about what a moving average is, and what an exponential moving average is, and what a range breakout system is, and what's in your charting. They get sucked into buying and selling, and a lot of times it's just one contract because that keeps the math simple. You can put it on a spreadsheet and off you go. You try different things, and you find something that you think works, and off you magically go and hope that you're successful.

Along the way of course I had my lessons that I'd learned on money management. I started driving home the point in spades that money management was far more important than the buying and selling stuff, but everybody that wanted to interview me as a potential money manager wanted to know about my trading strategy, not about my money management. The clients want to know more about what we're doing.

And I thought, what I need to do, is to once and for all shut up people about this nonsense of, "It's all about the trading strategy" and "It's not about the money management." I developed a strategy where I took our cleaned-up databases and five or six markets, maybe seven markets. It was replicated by some guys in Austria with about 20 or 30 markets. Same conclusion.

In my study I said, "Okay let's flip a coin, random number generator. At the end of the day if we don't have a position—if it's heads you buy, if it's tails you sell. As soon as that position's put in place, you take a simple range breakout strategy, and if it's a sell I put in a buy stop. If it's a buy I put in a sell stop." I move it in the same direction as the trade goes, so you're truly just letting the trade run as long as you can until it has to stop, and then you flip the coin again.

What I found when I did that was over any run I did, because it's random, over lots and lots of runs, it slightly made money. Not a lot, but it made money. And the key to it was balancing the portfolio perfectly. Each one of the seven positions had a meaningful impact on the portfolio. There wasn't one that was dominating, or one that was dominating good, one dominating bad. They were meaningful and all of the risk control was there with volatility control. We had the risk as a percent of equity limits, so we had all the number of contracts perfectly balanced. That's what creates the profits. The buying and selling don't make that much difference. You can use a coin flip and still make money.

The guys in Austria that ran it on 20 or 30 markets actually made more money per year than I did with my coin flip because I only had seven markets. They might have been running a little bit more portfolio heat in the end, but they had made money too.

Michael: A question from Guru Prasad; he's got a real simple question here within a larger question. He really wants to know about percent betting. He's saying he feels comfortable at 1% and I think he would really like to hear your view on percent of capital bet on each trade and maybe how you view that choice of percent bet.

Tom: This is where it's very important for each trader to do his own simulations on percents. We had limits, as I already said, on things like margin-to-equity, volatility-to-equity, risk-to-equity. We had those specific numbers that we had come to based on simulating how various leverages feed back into return streams and how the portfolio can go up and down in a particular day, week, month, year—what kind of maximum drawdowns do you tend to get out of different portfolio heat levels and how much leverage.

And so he's very perceptive. 1% is an area where we ran TrendStat quite a bit. In some cases, some markets we were down in less than 1%. Very rarely were we above it. And we had pretty much ongoing trade risks up in the 2% ranges because we had a position that was now moving in our direction. Our stops have now been moved, and we're starting to get to the point where we're going to start letting it run as far as we can, and a little more risk is fine.

Excessive risk then is not fine. I think that's a question that each trader needs to handle for himself. An important thing to note is now that I'm in retirement and I have my wife and myself as our sole two clients, and she's happy with what I'm doing, I can run the portfolio, especially my futures portfolio, a little bit higher than 1% and feel very comfortable with it. I know what I'm doing; I know it's going to go up and down a little bit more, but I know I've controlled the amount of risk that I've got, and that makes trading it a little bit faster not a big deal to me.

Michael: You want people to see what the range of possibilities are.

Tom: Correct. Each trader should try to simulate some trading ideas at different levels and try to dial it in probably a little lower than you think you can tolerate, because in the heat of the battle, when you're in that major drawdown that you never had before, having less of a drawdown will be better than having more of a drawdown. You want to err on the conservative side of the numbers. If you do your simulations and it comes out that you think you can do 2%, then maybe do 1.5% for a while, and see if you think that's okay. You don't need to be rushing out and trading 10% of your equity on a position.

Michael: Giuseppe Liuzzo asks, "How do you diversify your portfolio, Tom?"

Tom: That's a tough one. Globally we've gotten into so much electronic data, so many computers trading, so many different markets, it was easy for TrendStat to manage something like 30 currency forex markets, around 80 futures markets and about 25 mutual funds. We were able to trade those with 10 people. Four of those people were doing development work; they weren't managing it. Only two were involved in the actual production of orders and running up the trades. So two people are handling hundreds of clients across hundreds of different positions by scores of different strategies, and it's easy to do every day. I think the afternoon runs would take maybe 10 minutes in the case of currencies, and then we'd run the rest of it in maybe 15 minutes. It wouldn't take that long at all.

Diversification is harder and harder to come by though, because in any one day, let's say you take a soybean contract and you take a gold contract, theoretically those two shouldn't have a whole lot to do with each other. Gold could go up, and soybeans could go up; gold could go up and soybeans could go down—on and on, all the different possibilities. You would hope that by having a soybean and a gold in your portfolio, you would have some diversification.

But what's happened historically more and more, and it's always during times of major news announcements—wars breaking out, collapse of this, a bubble bursting, or whatever—you get what I call lockstep periods where every market moves in a direction that's either 100% correlated with another market, or 100% inversely correlated with another market and nothing in between. They're no longer independent. You look at your portfolio on a day when this major thing happens and all of a sudden your entire screen is green. Every position in your portfolio is green. You're making money across the board.

The very next day a shift happens and everything is red. You're at 100% lockstep, you've got no diversification. You think you do, but you don't.

The other situation I see a lot in the novice portfolios, they'll come in and say, "I want you to look at my portfolio." Okay, fine. It's some relative or a friend, and I'm looking at their portfolio. They've been sold by their broker or financial planner on numerous different gross stock mutual funds. I remember my sister had a portfolio she showed me, and it had five different mutual funds in the portfolio, three of which were just big old gross stock mutual funds. I said, "You don't have any diversification, and they're all going to go up when the market goes up, they're all going to go down when the market goes down. You're going to buy and hold them—that's not diversification." She said, "But I have three different ones." Well, that does not give you any diversification.

The answer to it is a difficult one. You're trying to grind through all the different markets and how they trade against other markets over a time period; but in the back of your mind, you're also trying to say to yourself, "When times of crisis exist and lockstep sets in on these markets, I'd better have my risk control schemes in place to limit my exposure, both good and bad unfortunately. I don't want the bad part of it to reside in my portfolio when I know that no matter what I do, I'm going to get zero diversification in the world as the markets are just so correlated these days."

Michael: Chris May asks sarcastically, "Where's gold going in the next six months?"

Tom: That's so cute.

Michael: Fred Penny has a good question: "What would cause you to stop trading a particular system? And then what might cause you to start trading that same system again?"

Tom: What would cause me to stop trading a strategy would be the day I realized that in market conditions existing in recent history, the results I got from that trading strategy were different than I would have expected given the way that strategy had gone through those markets. Something would have to have happened that I did not expect. That's why I was so big on going through the data day by day with a ruler in the simulations. I needed to understand everything that happened. How that strategy worked, how it reacted to various types of movements, so that as I'm going through life and looking at the last two weeks or three weeks or four weeks, seeing a market going one direction and it's not making any money, I can think to ask myself, "Why is it not making money? Something's wrong." *That's* what would cause me to stop trading a strategy and take a good look at it.

If I could find why it was doing *that* and where I was wrong on my construction of the strategy somehow—and feel comfortable in making some change to it that would solve that problem—then I would be immediately willing to start it up again. That is, I would start it up again if I went through the simulations and went through the line by line look on it and said, "This is ready for prime time. Let's get back into it."

If I couldn't find what was creating that anomaly between what I pictured to be the way it would act and the way it really acted, then I would just dismiss it, and it would go to the junk heap, and I'd move onto something new.

Michael: Were you always comfortable with the uncertainty that is always inherent in a strategy? So many want to believe that when they line up with their system to trade, they're going to get 1% a month, every month. I think anybody that starts to understand this world, this way of thinking, has to really find peace with uncertainty.

Tom: The way to do it is to look at daily returns or some large amounts of data. I had, I don't know, 20 or 30 years of cleaned-up data back in the day. We had huge databases that we could go through. When you start looking at daily data, or even weekly or monthly data, you're talking about so many data points. If you throw them on a bell curve or something, you're going to see a wide variety of different types of conditions.

I viewed my job as a money manager more as managing all this random data coming in and just making good money management decisions by dealing with all the data and not getting too emotionally involved in things like, "What did the gold market do today?" I don't really care. It's just another piece of data I had to process. That was maybe the good fortune of being more of a data processing mentality, a statistician mentality, an engineer mentality.

Michael: It's a puzzle for you to figure out.

Tom: Yeah. I have always treated money management and trading generally just like a puzzle. It's no different than trying to work out a sudoku, or a crossword puzzle, or solve something. Trading is a brain-teaser. It's a mental effort. It's like golf. You'll never achieve a perfect round of golf. Every time you get done, you say, "If I could have just made the putt on 17, I could have done this," and there's always a way to look ahead and say, "I can do better than this." Trading's the same way. You never arrive at the final destination, you only sort of get better at it over your lifetime, and then somewhere along the way you die, and you can't get any better. But you never achieve the final destination. You never become the perfect trader.

Michael: Howard Frazer wants your views on initial capital at risk versus unrealized gains.

Tom: My wide view is that when we did studies of return-to-risk at every point in a trend following trade, you could take every buy signal you got and say, "Okay, that is day zero. I am in the position now at this price. My stop is wherever it is," and then you go ahead, and you let the trade continue on, and you measure the risk per contract and the return. You calculate ahead and use your historical database to figure out what the final result of that trade ultimately is.

But then you go back and go through every day of the trade and figure out what the potential future return for the rest of that trade was versus the risk at that point in time. Let's say the trade's going to be 30 days long and you're going to make 10%. On day five, it's only going to be 25 days to go till you're out of it; it's only going to have a certain amount of return. It might not be 10%, it might be 7.5%, and then what is the risk at that point? And so we'd measure return-to-risk every single day throughout the entire trend following trade. We did this over hundreds and hundreds of trades.

We concluded without a doubt that the day you get into a trend following trade is the day when your return-to-risk ratio is the best. This relates to that question on pyramiding that someone asked. Pyramiding means you're getting in later in the trade and expecting it to continue to go your way. Your return-to-risk ratio is not as good with that pyramid trade. We pyramided or added positions, but we did them in very diminished quantity and under very stringent low-risk conditions. For example, we'd have a pullback or something, and we could move our stop up tight to the market. We would feel comfortable doing that and putting on a very small additional position.

That's a very tricky proposition to try to keep your return-to-risk ratios high enough to justify doing that. Now, to answer Howard's question, I always felt that when a market has gone in one direction and favors your position, you try to let those profits run. Let's say we are five days into this trade I just described, a 10% trade, and we're up 3% already. And so it's looking pretty good that this is going to be a profitable trade. You're already ahead nicely, and it's going your way. You don't know it's going to be 10%, but it's moving along good so far. The odds are now greater of having a profitable trade than not having a profitable trade if it moves in your direction. We did that study, too.

Given that, we loosened our risk and volatility controls a little bit for an existing trade—we called that *existing controls*. Then we had initial limits for the initial position. The existing trade levels were always a little higher than the initial risk levels and volatility levels. Use the 1% as an example. Say you need 1% risk with your portfolio and then maybe existing trades it's 2% risk of your portfolio, so you're giving it some room to grow.

Michael: I think you'd also make the point here once again that this is something where people need to not just trust Tom, but to test this—to see how the range of possibilities unfold.

Tom: Exactly. In the end, each trader has to live with his or her own decision. I'm not going to be there to console them, so they've got to come up with whatever level feels comfortable. I mean, with somebody like my mother, who couldn't stand to see her account go up or down a penny, she would have to trade like a tenth of 1% risk. Everybody's got their own level of comfort and I think you need to understand what that is.

For example, let's say Warren Buffett is going to go into trading 20 commodity markets. He's only going to put up $1 million to do that. Well, that's going to be such chump change of his total net worth. He might feel comfortable holding a different risk level because it's immaterial to him, even if he loses it all. His comfort level could be a lot different because of his situation. Comfort level also can come from expertise.

Michael: His utility of money is going to be different for sure, at his stage of the game.

Tom: Exactly. Also expertise levels. If somebody's very, very into their systems and understands exactly what they're doing and is comfortable with drawdowns generated by those strategies, well then you can run your risk levels a little higher perhaps. There's that technical expertise that you have over the novice. But the pure novice with no experience—keep it low. Just putting a trade on and taking it off even at a very low level may not be material for making a lot of money, but it's very material to your experience and your growth as a trader.

Michael: If I read you, Tom, you love giving insights about what you've experienced. The idea is that people can extrapolate from your knowledge and maybe get a little bit of a head start or learn from your experience .

But I don't think you are looking to hold yourself out as a guru. You're looking to be a man who's sharing his wisdom, sharing his insight, saying, "Here's my past experience." And I think the group of questions were pretty good. But there's some questions where you could tell people want the magic answer, and if you give them the magic answer then they're validated. That's really not what you're trying to get across to people. Is that a fair assessment?

Tom: It's a fair assessment. The only reason I put the direction that I have on my indicators and my hedges every day on my Facebook page is because I have a brother-in-law and a stepson who are trying to muddle through the early stages of trading. I find it convenient to communicate with them in that manner. They can actually find out which way I'm leaning to then ask me questions, which they usually do, and become more knowledgeable. I'm trying to help my stepson learn how to become a trader and manage his 401(k) and all that.

So I started posting on Facebook just for relatives and friends that were asking me the questions. It's dovetailed into about 300 friends all over the world, which I wasn't quite expecting at the time, but I don't mind carrying on the tradition.

Michael: Hopefully I'm responsible for eliminating some of the free time in your life.

Tom: It seems to be a lot of new friend requests usually have a Michael Covel as a mutual friend.

Michael: Imagine that. Okay, the last question I have for the day. Jeremy Clifford asks, "Do you have anything that you can think back on where the signal said, 'Get long or get short,' and your gut was saying, 'No way; this is insane,' but it's your system—you stuck with it, you did it, and it turned out to be a great winner?"

Tom: I've had those. One of them, I believe, was the market timing signal that I got to buy mutual funds off the bottom action after the '87 crash. I mean, the world was coming to an end. They were flooding liquidity in with the Fed, and we had lost 23% on the Dow in one day, something like that. And mutual funds fortunately were in cash about a week or two before the signal went off. Yet it was already a week before the crash actually hit.

I had preserved all the assets and now was getting a buy signal. I'm thinking to myself, "Boy, is this artificial. We've got the Fed coming in, we've got super volatility that's going off the map, but it's a buy signal and if this thing runs up, we're going to be caught without a position and it's not what we do." So I said, "It doesn't feel comfortable, but I'm doing it anyway." Turns out, if you bought in right after that crash, it did nothing but go up for a year or so. It was a good period. In situations like that, you just have to shake your head and go, "Oh boy, this will be interesting." But you've got to follow the strategy.

People at TrendStat had a role with me. I said, "As long as you do exactly what these computers tell you to do, I'll take the responsibility for the computers to be doing it correctly, and I'll also take the responsibility for having the strategy produce losses during any period. But you're going to take the responsibility of actually executing it flawlessly." By separating that out I relieved them of any stress of being wrong on the market direction or anything, and they could execute.

But yeah, I had a few times over my life that I've had that happen. Those times when you're most uncomfortable and so is almost everybody else out there—by the time everybody gets comfortable, the market's already moved significantly in that direction. You've got to turn your brain off a little bit and do the trade.

I try to encourage everybody to find their own way. List down what your resources are, what your skill levels are, what your mental capabilities are, how many dollars you are going to put into the thing, what markets you are trying to trade, and figure it out. Design what works for you. Because what works for you is not going to work for me, and what works for me is not going to work for you.

Brain Teasers

Michael: You're so good-natured. Is there a reason why Tom Basso is so good-natured? You sign a lot of your posts, "Enjoy the ride, my friends." That stands out as unusual in today's society.

Tom: When I was going through high school, I ended up observing my own behavior quite a bit. It was a weird thing where I almost had this second part of my brain that would watch what Tom Basso did every day. It gave me the ability to analyze how I reacted to the world around me, day after day. I used to do it once a day. I would think through the day and say, "Did I react well to that situation? Was I overly nervous or overly excited, overly depressed, or overly scared?"

As time went on through college, where I played a lot of basketball, I started noticing being able to be, sort of, out of my own body. I could almost look at our defense and call out where everybody was supposed to be and could see guys behind me. I could, in my mind, keep track of the other five guys, and realize there's one missing, so he's got to be behind my vision. Just stuff like that.

As I expanded and got into the real world, I realized that I took that attitude with life in general. It's like a movie, and I'm just flowing with it, and trading is one part of my life. So is hitting golf balls, cooking dinner, eating dinner, watching television, being a husband to my wife, and all the other things that go on with life. To make trading your whole world seems a bit shallow to me. There's so much more to life, and it's so short.

You get reminded of that as you get older. I'm 61 now. You start seeing some of your friends pass away. And you start realizing that it's nice to take some time to go to Tahiti. I was making arrangements for it this morning actually. To me, I only have a finite time on this earth, but trading will go on hopefully way past my lifetime, and it's nice to pass along the simple things I've learned that aren't rocket science. As you know from your knowledge of trend following, it's not that difficult. People make it difficult. If you can help people understand how simple it is and how there's more to life than just trading, I think that's a good thing. More balance in the world.

Michael: I caught a line where you talked about the idea of imagining. Imagining the horror, even if it doesn't happen—imagining feeling it. I thought to myself: stoicism.

Tom: Was this a reference to preparation?

Michael: Right. You've got to go through mental exercises and you were talking about the imagining. My first thought was stoicism because I always think of stoicism as, "Think through the worst-case scenarios, live them, live them in your mind, and then when some of these bad things happen you're not so surprised."

Tom: That's exactly right. I'd also argue that you should live through the good times as well in your mind. When you're getting into a position, if you can say, "If this went insane, like if tomorrow, this stock I just bought gets an offer for twice the value that I just put into it, what does that mean? How do I react? Am I overly excited, adrenalized? Do I want to take the profit, or am I just going to follow my strategy and just do what I do?"

You've got to prepare yourself for all sides of it. Not just the bad ones, but the good ones too. You have to think ahead, go through a lot of different scenarios, and be prepared mentally to deal with them.

Michael: That's trend following in the emotional arena as well.

Tom: It really is.

Michael: Since we started going down the psychology side of things, tell me some more about your mental exercises. I'm assuming the mental exercises, whether you're driving in the car or whatever else, are for far more than just trading.

Tom: I've played all sorts of games on myself over my lifetime with my brain, and I think that it reaped some good rewards. I already mentioned the observer self that I had in high school and through college. As I observe myself doing things, I think eventually somewhere—probably after college—this observer part of my brain dedicated itself to keeping track of what I was doing every day and meshed right into my brain. It became such a natural thing for it to be there, I don't even think about it. I don't see it as a separate entity.

There are all sorts of exercises that you can play with your mind. For instance, I remember Van Tharp saying that young boys who were about ready to go out and fight their first tiger or try to hunt their first lion would be taught to defocus their vision and see what it does to your brain. The psychology being that it takes away a lot of your fear.

I tried doing that on a golf course to some success, where I'm walking down a fairway looking at a distant object, but then after focusing my eye on a distant object like the pin, I try to see my peripheral vision clearly as well, so that the whole thing becomes this monster view going into my brain. You're not focused on any one thing, like that lake over to the right that your ball could go into if you hit it poorly. It's just this one big vision, and fear goes away.

Just being an observer is a lot of it. Driving, I've played games with just wondering how these guys get off the drag race when the light goes green. I'll be sitting there, and I'm watching everybody else who's playing with their texting and listening to the radio. I'm sitting there in the first position at an intersection, of course, being careful to look both ways, making sure nobody's coming at me. Trying to see what would be the quickest possible reaction time that my body can take my foot off the brake and put it on the gas. Not to go fast, but just to be the first car moving into the intersection, leaving the rest of them still wondering what's going on. Just little things like that. It's been fascinating to me learning how the human body works and how the brain works.

Michael: Even though we can't get into the minutiae of all these different types of things in this conversation, if anything, you can inspire people that are younger to think more about this mental aspect of success.

Tom: If you don't have mental capability and good psychology in trading, everything else you do will be destroyed. I could automate a program, put it in a black box, hand it to somebody who is a basket case mentally, and they will screw it up, because they don't have good control of their mind. They are going to have a problem even executing a well-constructed black box without screwing it up. They will override it, or not do a trade that they should've done. They'll take profits too quick because they finally feel like they've got all this profit built up, and they don't wait for their stop signal to get hit. It'll never be successful.

As soon as people realize that the mental side of trading is first and foremost, and last and least important is what you buy and sell, or where you buy and sell, then they have a chance at success.

Michael: There are plenty of super-successful traders who are not necessarily sure how they got there—maybe they had a little luck. Very wealthy people can make those mental errors you're talking about, and a life's fortune can go down very fast.

Tom: It certainly does. If you look at the first *Market Wizards* book and even the second one, you'll see certain people in there that are no longer around. They might have done well up to then, but they were pushing the envelope. They didn't have their mental processes screwed on as straight as they would've liked and went awry along the way. I survived 30 years, roughly, trading. If you want to count now, it's another 10 years trading currencies with no issues blowing up. I'm still doing it. It's been a long run.

You've got a lot of traders that don't make it that long. A lot of it is due to how they think through the process of how much risk they want to take on and how much they can stay with something day after day, after day, after day. I've always been pretty calm toward the whole thing, which is reflected in my trading. Some have accused me of being a little bit on the boring side in terms of trading. I never went for the fancy profits or anything. But I like to try to avoid the losses and continue to plug along. I think that serves you well over the long run. A lot of people could take a good lesson from that.

Michael: You're one of my most popular guests, if not the most popular. So your "boring" must be pretty exciting to a lot of people. That's my impression.

Tom: Every time we do one of these interviews, I get about 15 emails or Facebook messages.

Michael: Let me jump into some trading issues. I had a couple points that people brought up and a couple of things of my own. I saw a line that I want to read to you, and have you tell me what you think about it. The quote was this: "If you're not afraid of losing small amounts of money, you're almost invincible." How does that strike you?

Tom: It strikes me pretty well. If you do the statistics on what we did at TrendStat back over the years, various buy/sell programs that we had that ranged from perhaps 28% reliable all the way up to maybe 40%, but more realistically, 36%, 37% reliable. Averaging around 33%, or one-third, let's say. That means every single trade I get into, I've got a two-thirds chance of losing money.

If I take that on mentally and say, okay, I've got thousands of data points to tell me that I'm going to get two losses for every one gain. I might as well take the attitude that I've got to limit those two losses and be okay with it, because that's just two out of the three that I've got to look for. For every three trades I do, I'll get a profit and that profit will be bigger than the losses. I'll make money over the long run. That's what we're doing here, so why would I be concerned over those small losses? I think once you realize *that*, accept it, and understand why you've got to have those two losses, then you're well on the way to making some good money.

I heard one person say a long time ago, "Trading is sort of like breathing—everybody wants to breathe in because you get oxygen, but you have to breathe out also." That's kind of like the losses. They're both part of the breathing process, you've got to have in and out.

Michael: As I continue my yoga practice, I've learned that breathing is the core. It's the core of it all. Let me shift to another one. I did an interview today, and someone asked me a question that I'm going to give back to you. They wanted to know why trend following does so well when the black swans hit.

Tom: Trend following by its very math is saying, "Let your profits run as far as they want to run, and cut your losses short when they don't go your way." When a black swan happens, which is an outlier event of major consequence that has never happened before and has gone way beyond the realms of anything anybody's ever seen, trend following at some point is going to pick up or move in that direction. It may be a big gap to get into it, it may have started out months ago as nothing, and then all of a sudden has become a speculative bubble at this point. Every one will have a different way of starting. I've seen a number of them in my lifetime.

But no matter where you do get in, you will get in, and you will ride part of that black swan. That one trade and maybe a couple of others might be the difference between making money that year and losing money that year, when you take everything else and add it together. Your small gains are going to offset some of your small losses, but to really make money, you need those real outlier events. The kind of event that really drives a Japanese yen position you're in for a whole year, or a year and a half, and the thing has gone up 100% on the face value of the currency. You're leveraged, and you end up making hundreds or thousands of percent. That really pays the freight for a whole lot of losses, and that's why trend following makes money.

Michael: Let's talk about your daily routine. I caught a post the other day on your Facebook where you were talking about the total amount of time that it took to execute your daily routine. I have a feeling routine is very important in your life, and there's a reason why routine is very important. I want you to explain the time that it takes for you, now that you have your system and your daily execution in place.

Tom: Let's talk about the two things. First, time. The other day, I posted something, and I think it took me 12 minutes after the markets closed to go through my entire process. I forget exactly the numbers, but I want to say I moved about four stops in the stock area times four accounts. I think I moved one or two futures trades … I can't remember how many. I also checked and moved some stops on my hedge trades, and it all took me 12 minutes. I did that because I was getting some posts and questions from traders on how much they need to do and how often they need to look at the market. I was getting the reaction that some of these people were spending their entire day looking at the screen. I'm thinking to myself, "What could I possibly do to waste that much time?"

I timed myself, to make the point to everybody out there that sure, if you want to argue about it, I've got 28 years at TrendStat, another 10 years retired, honing my skills.

Michael: Hold on, that's not even 40 years yet. That's only 38 years.

Tom: It's only 38 years. I'm still only 61. But when you get that much experience under your belt, you know what you've got to do every day. You just have to execute it. If you're trying to design a new way of trading every single day and every single moment, looking at the screen and looking at the price going up and down is going to just gobble up time and it's so non-productive. Constantly asking, "What does this tell me? Should I change my strategy? Should I do some research on this new idea that I just heard in a podcast or a newsletter or got from a friend?" You're going through all this gyration in your mind.

In my case, I know exactly what I've got to do to execute my trend following models. I pull up my screens and, starting at the top, I begin going click, click, click, click. Of course, I'm faster and faster over the years with my mouse and my computers, and I know exactly what I've got to do next, so I keep going without hesitation. I try to tell my wife, "I'm going to be closing the market down," and she knows to just stay away from the office for a little bit. Twelve minutes later, I was done, stopped the clock, and I went and did the Facebook post. That's where the time thing came from.

But routine, as you mentioned, is important. I got the routine side of things from the standpoint that the markets will wait for no one. That is one of the things I always told my staff at TrendStat. That's why we had so many backups. If somebody's taking a vacation, somebody else has to fill their spot. The markets won't shut down because you're having a Fourth of July. Because guess what—London does not respect the US's Fourth of July. We revolted from them. The currency markets are open on the Fourth of July. We've got to be there, we've got to still do our thing. Who's going to take a vacation day, who's going to work?

Routine becomes something that is driven by the way the markets work, and really almost all of life. You get up and it's probably good to have breakfast in the morning, because it fuels your body for the rest of the day. It's probably good to exercise. I see you upside-down sideways in your yoga positions, and you're obviously in good shape. I could not do that, wouldn't even try. But I do work out. I am in good shape for a 61-year-old, I think, and still hitting the golf ball pretty well. I'm enjoying all these things.

I think that routine of exercising, eating, hydrating your body with water, and making sure you're there for the markets is essential. I've got to put my stops in and move my stops or check things once a day. On this cruise to Tahiti, for instance, that we were talking about earlier, I'm now up to a level with this cruise line where they give me unlimited internet on the concierge level, which is where I'm going to be. I'll bring along the computer, and sometime each day after the markets close in Tahiti, I will be on my computer for my 12 minutes. Then I will go back to having fun. There's a certain routine that has to be done. Some people think that's too rigid, but I can spare 12 minutes on a vacation. I don't think of that as too burdensome.

Michael: Especially with the life freedom that you get from making the choices that you've made. Some people think, "I'm going to go on vacation, I don't want any distraction." But those are the same people that go back and work a nine-to-five grind for the bossman their entire lives. So I agree with you completely.

Tom: Or they go back home and they find that they've missed all sorts of signals that they should've gotten. Remembering the story I told Jack Schwager back when he was doing the *New Market Wizards* interview with me about the silver trade. My parents were visiting me, I had missed the silver trade, and it turns out it was worth $100,000. This was when my account was $10,000, and I had missed it. And I missed it because I wasn't paying attention to my stuff; I was playing tour guide to my parents. I'm not blaming my parents, it's my responsibility. I should've been taking my 12 minutes, or whatever it was back then, to do my work. I got sloppy, missed the trade, missed that profit. That would've put me way ahead of where I ended up being now. I would've been that much farther ahead at an earlier stage and been profitable earlier in my trading.

You have to really look at how you go through every day and ask yourself, "Where does the time slip away?" Because you wake up in the morning, go to sleep at night, and there're a lot of minutes in between. If you really think about what you spend those minutes on, it's amazing how many you can waste.

Michael: In this day and age we waste a lot of time with all these electronic gadgets.

Tom: Absolutely.

Michael: This is a good question from Fred Penny. He says, "If you were a 20-something guy or gal today without much money and looking back with your experience, would you approach trading the same way?"

Tom: I don't think so. I ended up, as most people know, a money manager, a futures trader, and a currency trader. TrendStat Capital was my firm before we shut it down back in 2003.

When I started, if you could just establish that you were trading even $100,000 and doing it successfully over a period of, say, one, two, three years, and maybe showed growth and assets from $100,000 maybe to a half a million, people would take a serious look at you. They might say, "This guy's making progress. His track record looks solid. I like his approach. He seems sensible. He seems like a smart businessman. He's hiring people to back him up. He's got computer equipment. Yeah, we'll give him a chance. Here's another $5 million." Now all of a sudden you've got $10 million under management, and somebody will give you another $10 million and pretty soon you're at $20 million, and then you're off to the races, and you can build your business that way.

Nowadays, I'm a little bit removed from the industry, being retired, but I've heard stories where some asset allocators would want you to have $20 million or $50 million under management and have a staff of 10 people, computer equipment, backup locations, marketing staff, and everything else. I don't know if I would've ever gotten into the business with all of that.

I'd be inclined to go ahead and work, as you said before, a nine-to-five job of some sort. Perhaps one that had a little bit of flexibility to it, so that I could do some trading as I was working the job. When I was a chemical engineer, I could easily go home at 4:30 from designing chemical plants and spend half an hour working on my commodity account and transmit my orders, and then go have dinner. It wasn't a big deal.

Michael: Your real issue, if I'm hearing you, is it's the money management versus the trading. They're not one and the same.

Tom: No, they are not. For those people who think they're going to get into the money management industry, let me tell you that the year before I shut TrendStat down, I spent $100,000 on regulatory CPA and legal fees at no benefit to my clients that I could see. I spent probably 60% of my time either with personnel, accounting, or legal issues, and less than 10% of my time actually doing meaningful research or trading that most people would think is the fun thing that they like to do. You spend very little time trading, more time running a business, if you want to be successful at it.

If it was me right now, I probably would've stayed an engineer for longer, or moved into the business side of the company I was at. I probably would've done a little more strategic planning and business. I was highly rated at this company I was at. I was promoted a month before I quit. They seemed to like what I was giving them and doing. I would just get more raises there, get into stock options, get into whatever you can get into, and keep saving a lot of that money. Put it into your trading accounts. Hone your skills at smaller amounts of money and then get your portfolio to the point where it is supplying an extra source of income for you.

And when that extra source of income got to the point where it was equal to your employment income, you probably could safely retire at that point. I would guess that, rather than retiring at 51 had I done that, I might've been able to retire even earlier, because the things that I did at TrendStat, by their nature, had to be very regulatory. For instance, I couldn't front run or anything like that. I had to be careful with what positions I had versus the clients' positions, and all these things. Basically, I had to keep everything pretty plain vanilla with my own trading, to match my clients. Or I actually put my money in the same fund that my clients are in, so that I'm getting exactly the same trades, in essence, so that there would be no favoritism to me or the clients, because that's illegal.

I think without those restrictions, what I'm finding after 10 years of retirement is I can do things that I could never do for clients. I trade orange juice futures. Gee, I only need one or two of them for my portfolio. If I had TrendStat with $600 million under management, how am I going to buy orange juice futures? I might be able to buy 10 or 20 of them, but that's not going to mean anything to my clients. It's a whole different world when you're trading for yourself.

Michael: You mentioned the regulatory environment. I'm not purporting to be a regulatory expert, but it is worth stating that not all regulatory climates are the same. I'm not saying one country's regulation is bad and another's is good. I'm just saying that there are some places where the regulation has gotten a little tougher than others.

Tom: There are some places that are easier, and some places that are actually worse than the US, in some ways—very, very ancient thinking on certain things. And some states in the US are worse than other states. Wisconsin comes to mind as a state that seems to have extremely stringent restrictions on mutual funds and things like that. They seem to always have a tough time getting people to blue sky their stuff.

Michael: I wouldn't make assumptions that everything within each climate is the same, or that all countries are the same.

Tom: Sadly, some of the friends I have on Facebook that live around the world—they're in Australia, Vietnam, or someplace—realize, as I did, that a lot of the assets you can obtain to manage seem to be in the US. We are a very wealthy country and there are a lot of assets, a lot of pension plans, that need to be managed here. When I got into the currency business it got a little bit better because there was less regulation on currency trading. There were banks like Royal Bank of Canada, Bank of Montreal, Soc. Gen over in France, and other places that I had as clients where I didn't have the regulation and they weren't in the US and having to deal with US stuff either.

I had some US banks as clients; I had some foreign banks as clients. It was an interesting mix. Different environments are definitely to be explored, because how you run a business is all going to be about what you're allowed to do. The government and your clients restrict the money manager and what he or she is able to do day to day managing the portfolio, so that is going to dictate some of your success. If your clients and regulation don't let you buy orange juice futures, then it can't be part of your portfolio. It's just a simple fact. That does affect your returns. You have to think about *that*.

Michael: Let me shift gears on you. I love shifting gears on you. Why not, right?

Tom: Why not? That's why I like your interviews. I never know where they're going.

Michael: Do you tinker with your current systems? And how do you know when you're dealing with a normal drawdown versus, "Oh-oh, this system is shot!"

Tom: I'm currently, in my futures trading, using the same buy and sell triggers that I think I created and probably was using back in about 1984.

Michael: How ancient. How archaic. They can't be useful. They can't be good anymore, Tom. You've got to retire those!

Tom: They're virtually identical. The only difference is I used to do it all on graph paper, but now I have computers. I'm now looking at fancy colors and all sorts of data that I didn't have available, so it's a little easier.

Michael: So the graph paper would take you from 12 minutes to 30 minutes?

Tom: I used to take about an hour doing my futures portfolio. My goal over my lifetime was actually to put myself out of work so that I could have more time to golf and do other things.

Michael: We've established that you don't tinker.

Tom: No, but I do make enhancements. Let's take an example—ETFs were not around in the past. Back in the day, I traded mutual funds. We'd look for no load mutual funds and we'd have to do end-of-day buy and sell, because that's the nature of a mutual fund.

When ETFs came into being and traded continuously throughout the day, then you could start thinking about stop orders and intraday execution. To me, this minimized the risk of the overnight gap and therefore was a good thing to add to my portfolio.

I wouldn't call that necessarily tweaking, as much as looking at various new products that might come into the portfolio. I might have to do something a little different to actually try to physically trade those, but the ones that I've had in the past, I don't tweak too much.

Michael: How about drawdowns? If the drawdown starts to be a little steep, how do you know when things are going too far?

Tom: This is the scenario analysis we were talking about earlier. With your strategy, you should think through: "If this thing goes well and I have these types of market conditions, this is what's going to happen. This is what's going to happen if it goes really to crap, and this is what's going to happen if we have an expected month or six months."

If you've really thought about that and done a good job of it, then you should ask yourself on a drawdown, "What are the markets being traded? What does your portfolio look like? What market action has been provided to you by the market?" You have nothing to do with any of those things. That was just the universe giving you ups and downs and sending you all over the place.

Next, ask yourself, "Given those conditions, would you have expected anything different than what you're seeing?" If the answer is yes, then I would say something's wrong with your strategy, and you need to do some tweaking. You need to do some research to find out what the difference is between what you would've expected versus what actually happened.

But if you answer that same question, "This is an extraordinarily choppy period, and there's been some violent disruptions that I would get caught in with this strategy, and I would expect to have a drawdown," then it's not broken—don't fix it.

Michael: Straightforward.

Tom: That's how I look at it.

Michael: Jim Byers has a question. He was curious if you are a one-system guy, or multiple systems?

Tom: Multiple. When I was at TrendStat and running our flagship fund, Market Math, we had six different portfolios within the fund that ranged from trading commodity options to two different approaches in currencies, two different approaches in futures, and one approach to mutual fund timing. Within the mutual fund timing even, there were two different sub-pieces to that. And in one of the futures areas, there're probably a couple sub-pieces there. These were all trend following, in a way, but they were all very different in their approach.

Michael: Ultimately, they all got to trend following, but in different ways.

Tom: Yes—based on the markets, based on what I was trying to accomplish, based on how much risk that particular portfolio was trying to take on. Some of the strategies we had—particularly the ones that were, for example, 28% reliable—you've got more losses that you're going to take as a percentage of the total. Because they're 28% reliable, the math would say you've got to have a bigger gain when you have a gain, and the losses could be bigger as well.

Other strategies were more, "Just catch every intermediate move up and down and don't worry about the big one, we'll be there for it. If we get whipsawed along the way, so what? The big guy next door will pick up the big gain and not get whipsawed." We'd have different personalities to these trading strategies. Some clients would pick and choose and say, "I like that; I don't like that."

If you got in Market Math, then it was my decision as to how it was all allocated. We did a lot of research on that and how much exposure we wanted to each of the strategies, and then we rebalanced that monthly back to the set point. It was the Robin Hood approach of taking from the wealthy strategy and giving to the poor strategy. Whatever was in a drawdown was being fed, and whatever was on an explosive up move, with equity coming in like crazy, we're taking money off of the table. That stabilized everything and kept us with a nice steady performance.

Michael: We're in an interesting economic climate. Everybody can hear the political debates, regardless of the side of the fence you're on. Some folks want more government, some folks want less government. I know where you fall on the spectrum; we probably have very, very similar views.

Can you paint a picture—from your perspective, watching markets evolve, watching governments evolve, and especially watching the Fed's involvement—for people that don't have your time horizon lens? How do you see what's going on today in terms of Fed action? It seems to me we're in brave new territory. Are we? Or is it just some of the same that we've seen over the decades?

Tom: Well, I might back up from just the Fed to something just slightly bigger than that, in that society in general these days seems to be gravitating down. And certainly the Fed is doing the same thing along this line of not taking responsibility for themselves. You've taken the responsibility, for instance, to go to Vietnam, to go to Asia and to do your speaking, to bootstrap a business out of your podcasts and be successful.

I think that took a lot of work and a lot of courage. The average person, when they're in front of the television every night, and they can get a government stipend of some sort or maybe can get an unemployment benefit and not have to go out and look for a job tomorrow, or say "It's kind of cold tomorrow, I think I'll stay in." I think, second by second, minute by minute, there's this tendency to think that government and the big entities are going to take care of all these little individuals.

And the individuals kind of allow them to do that, strangely, because it's the easy way to go. Rather than the difficult way that you've gone or that I've gone. It's easy to not take responsibilities. It's easy to say, "Somebody else is at fault for the way that my little life is today." I think the Fed is sitting there saying, "We've got an economy that's being overburdened by a government that's spending more than it takes in. We've got $17 trillion in actual debt, we've got $100 trillion in unfunded liabilities. That adds up to about $117 trillion. The GDP of the country is only about $15 or $16 trillion a year, so that's multiple years of total 100% GDP to even get close to this huge liability number." That's not a good recipe for success. I can't imagine how any economist could put a good spin on that, although the Keynesians seem to try.

The reality of it is, the Fed is saying, "What other choice do we have?" If the stock market were to crash, if commodities start skyrocketing, if we have unabated inflation, if we have a depression, or whatever it is, it's going to spill over to the entire world. It could get really rough. There're going to be riots in the streets and all sorts of problems. I hate to be negative, so you try to look at the positive side in that and you try to say, "Okay, let's see if we can keep funding enough money into this thing to keep it muddling along somehow."

Over time, maybe somebody brilliantly figures a way out of the mess, but it's looking pretty dismal. The Fed has used so many different tools so far, and I think they're running out of arrows in the quiver. I don't know what they're going to be able to do going forward if things get tough. I would remain very cautious toward your trading. I would also look, like you have, at other countries and diversify internationally if you can. Do what you can to protect yourself, because I think times could get a little interesting going forward.

Michael: Some may say, "Why does Tom Basso have this opinion?" or "Why does Mike Covel have this opinion about the markets? Who cares?" It's gotten so unusual. If you don't have a public policy view, regardless of what your trading is, I start to wonder what's wrong with you. Not you, Tom, but this has gotten so unusual out there that if you don't have a view, it scares me.

Tom: One of the most profound things that happened to me along the way was this ability to listen to someone talking and separate fact from opinion and flag them in my brain. When you're reading a *Wall Street Journal* article where some panelist is saying, "I think this, and the market's going to be here, and that's my prediction," you just flag it and say, "Okay, that's interesting, but it's just an opinion." And when Tom says something or Michael says something, that's just their opinion.

However, if I say, "The market closed at 183.76 today," or whatever number it is, that is an actual data point. That's a fact. That's not my opinion; it is just a number. I think once you start separating facts and data from people's opinions, the whole world of trading gets a whole lot clearer. In my mind, I could think the world's going to come to an end, go to hell in the next year, and I could still be long in the market. I really don't have any other choice.

I mean, where else are you going to put your money and where else are you going to try to hold onto some value with the Fed devaluating the dollar by pumping so much money into the system? You're probably going to end up having to make 10% and 20% returns just to try to hold yourself even in terms of purchasing power, and that's a pretty daunting task.

Michael: Strange days indeed. But I love hearing your wisdom, and I know others do too.

Travel, Politics and Catastrophic Events

EPISODE 306: JANUARY 1, 2015

Michael: How are you?

Tom: I'm doing fantastic. Just got back from two weeks in French Polynesia and very relaxed. I'm taking a break from moving five tons of gravel in my yard right now to talk to you, and then I'll go back to that when we're done.

Michael: The five tons of gravel sounds like good exercise to say the least.

Tom: That's the way I view it.

Michael: French Polynesia? I've not been there, though I've been in roughly that same part of the world. It's probably another 10 hours from where I've been in Southeast Asia.

Tom: About, yes. It's in the southern hemisphere just off New Zealand. It's pretty far south. Although it's their summertime right now, so 80s, humid, probably a lot like Vietnam and some other places in the summer.

Michael: Could you live in a place like that?

Tom: Not out of choice, but I could live there if I had to. But I really enjoy Arizona a lot. It has the best of it all—the mountains, peace and quiet, beautiful trees. And then it's got the desert down in the valley, the Phoenix area, where there's a lot of action—concerts, plays, restaurants and things to do. They're only 90 minutes away from each other, so I have the best of both worlds.

Michael: On to trading. I've seen in the headlines there've been some hedge funds that have not had the greatest returns this year. A lot of people are bemoaning the price of oil. It's kind of funny. You would think, "Oil drops—everyone should be happy." But apparently there are so many budgets and social programs tied to high oil around the world, so a lot of people aren't happy. But hey, this is a zero-sum game, so quite a few people in our little world are happy that oil has dropped.

What's so interesting is how many people, five, six, seven months ago were talking about a 50% crater in oil. Nobody was predicting this at all, but then there's one trading strategy that seemed to do exceptionally well during this unpredictable run.

Tom: Yeah. Trend following. And all you have to do is short at some place up around the 100 or 90, and enjoy the ride.

Michael: You make it sound so simple. I saw the head of OPEC said, "All the speculators are doing this." I said, "Hold on, at what price are the speculators not involved in oil?"

Tom: They're involved in every single price. The reason speculators are in there is because they help to create a price. Without the speculators there and the constant buying and selling, we wouldn't know where the price of oil is from second to second. You might know where it was from day to day or maybe even hour to hour as large companies and large hedgers make a transaction, but the market would be very inefficient. It would jump all over the place.

With speculators there we can have trades going off every second, and you know exactly where the price of oil is second by second.

Michael: I know you personally don't ponder these things so much because you've been there, done that, and you understand it deep in your gut. But when you hear a headline where the head of OPEC is saying that the price is where it should not be, the fundamentals do not support this price and cast blame at speculators for this particular point in price, explain to the audience just how disingenuous that is.

Tom: It's disingenuous because the price of anything is where someone will buy and sell it. If a speculator would be selling it and driving the price down, someone else has to be buying it to make that transaction happen. The person buying it could also be a speculator. How can speculators be driving it down if speculators are on both sides of that trade? Or it could have been a hedger—let's say Southwest Airlines in the past has come in and bought gas when they thought it was cheap. Maybe they're thinking that now, so maybe the speculator's selling it to Southwest, and they're hedging their future fuel costs.

All right, fine. Then, it goes down cheaper. Southwest can buy some more future cheap oil. Nobody ever complains, especially OPEC, when the prices go skyrocketing up to 100, but the same speculators are there at that point in time as they are right now. Speculators don't just short the market; they go both ways. It's for public relations to try to place blame. They are trying to placate their people because Saudi Arabia depends so much on oil, as does Norway. Norway, I think, has some socialistic types of programs out there in the countries that depend on oil. Brazil too, to some extent, as well as Venezuela.

All countries that are leaning toward liberal socialist programs and using oil revenues to try to help pay for them don't have those revenues anymore to the level that they used to, so they try to place blame. They try to not point the finger at themselves for setting up a religion that was based on a house of cards, but that's the way the world works these days it seems.

Michael: I was in Dubai over the weekend. When you talk about when the price of oil is high and no one complains, I know why they're not complaining. I saw what they have been building with that oil money over there. They've done a fabulous job building out a city. I don't know if it's where I'd want to live, but they've done a hell of a job.

Tom: I've seen the photos on your Facebook page. They're very impressive.

Michael: Let's talk about your stomach lining for a second. I think this is a good reminder for everyone—whether it's the professional, the new trader, or the new investor—to talk about Tom Basso's stomach lining. And if you don't mind also, the rush and the devastation.

We can have this emotional rush of, "Oh my gosh, I'm making so much money," and then, "I'm losing money—the devastation."

Tom: First of all, my stomach lining seems to be doing just fine as far as I can tell. I have never had any ulcers or anything else; knock on wood, I guess. In my early trading years there were some silver trades that went all over the place. That really was catching my attention almost hour by hour.

That opens your eyes a lot. I realized out of that, that there's no reason you can't stay true to trend following and stay with the position. You just need to manage the position size. All I did was figure out ways to volatility adjust and to risk adjust my positions throughout a trade, so things would become fairly tame and the stomach lining would be kept intact. There was nothing to get excited about, because one day was roughly the same as every other day.

That's what I learned out of the early trading mistakes and situations where it really would have gotten to my stomach lining over my lifetime. But once I got to TrendStat, we just automated a lot of that to the point where it just happened automatically. The only thing that would affect my stomach lining at that point would be a power outage, or the internet lines going down, or the program not working properly. But it certainly wasn't the markets anymore.

Michael: You've talked about how you would mentally rehearse catastrophic events and also if you've got a position on and it's the wrong kind of position. If you're long, and you don't adjust, and oil drops 50%, that's a catastrophic event. I saw a great comment from Van Tharp where he talked about having a phone call from you once, and you said that you had a disaster the prior day and you couldn't answer the phone. You couldn't talk to Van. But basically he said it was a planned disaster.

Even as a young man you were thinking, "How do I plan for catastrophic events? How do I plan for the unexpected?" Because it's going to happen.

Tom: Right. I was amazed at how many CTAs and other professional traders did not plan for disasters. We would once a year at least have what I would call a disaster day, and I would tell everybody ahead of time. Everybody in the company knew what to expect and I asked a little bit extra out of everybody. We moved a section of the company to our offsite location to operate in an alternative mode. We tried to run the company from the secondary location while a certain number of people stayed in the primary location to answer phone calls from clients and things that would come in that would be normal routine business. We didn't want to have our disaster day exercise affecting the clients being able to get to us and schedule appointments or talk to us or something.

With Van's conference, that wasn't absolutely necessary, so I put him off. I was trying to make sure we did this exercise and it required a whole lot of attention, particularly because when you're operating backup equipment it's a little bit more clunky than it would be with your mainstream stuff.

What we did all day was offloaded data to the backup facility; then we put orders in from the backup facility. We tried to call our trading desk from the backup facility, we tried to look at procedures, and we made sure to have all the Word files and Excel spreadsheets that we needed to operate.

Invariably, what you get out of those exercises is a good list of things that you missed or that have changed since last time you did a disaster backup, and you can improve and tighten your operations. I find it amazing that some CTAs just have a single operation, and they don't have a clue what would happen if, say, the mobile phones went down or if the internet went down.

There are so many different scenarios. If you've actually gone through some of them and tried to tell your trading partners what you're doing, I always found that they were very, very excited in working with me to generate ways of operating in an emergency because they have the same problem on their side. They want to know that I'm going to be able to deal with what happens to me, and in some of these cases they were giving us money to trade, so we were trying to be good partners.

That's something that we can do in a lot of aspects of life. It's amazing how many people let life put it to them. Then there's the stress of dealing with it, as opposed to trying to say, "Well I could go this way and those following two and three things could happen, or it might not happen and it might be this, and if it is, do I go to plan B or do I try to solve that problem?"

There're a lot of things you can do if you think ahead a little bit, do a little planning, do a little exercising, and then it's not so stressful when it happens.

Michael: Those catastrophic events though—it's not necessarily only what you've just described. It's also about your portfolio, your trading strategy.

Tom: Sure it is. And to some extent probably the most catastrophic move that I ever saw was when we invaded Iraq during H. W. Bush, when we went from Kuwait into Iraq. Those years, when I was closing down the markets, I think oil was at $32 a barrel; we were long. By 8 p.m. that night we had had a bit of a computer issue at TrendStat, and I was staying late. I left having solved the problem at about 8 p.m., which would have been six hours or more after the close, and oil was up to $40 a barrel, and we were going into Iraq. So I thought, "This ought to be pretty nice." I go to sleep and I come in the next day, and oil is at $22 a barrel and we're stopped out and take a chunk of a loss. I think we lost about 5% or 6% of the whole portfolio that day which was, to that day and to this day, the largest single-day loss that I saw in the trading of futures markets.

We made it back and we were at new highs two or three months later. It wasn't a big deal, but wow, 6% in one day, that's interesting. It wasn't something that was unusual because we saw what the markets did. It was a bad day, but we could recover from a 6% loss; it's not going to hurt you, and we had managed that position properly. It had gotten very volatile, so we were down to minimum-sized positions. When it got down to $22, a lot of accounts couldn't even own a position because the volatility was too great. We would keep them out of a position altogether. Life was good, and we, like I said, came back to new highs shortly thereafter.

Michael: It sounds so simple, but I think for most people that simple story can go right over their head. The big-picture point is that you're saying, "Hey look, we've got to have chips to play the game. Our egos are not so big that we know what's going to happen next, so if the market's not going our way, let's take our losses, get out, and come back to play another day."

Tom: Exactly right. That's all it is. It's how do you get to your next 1,000 or 2,000 or 10,000 trades? It's all a matter of statistics. Any one trade can either win or lose.

Michael: In every piece of media—and of course media's not relevant to trend following trading—whether it's print, radio, online, TV, it's all about the trade for that day. But with trend following you need to look more big picture and calmly and coolly say, "Hey, hold on, I don't care about one trade, I care about 1,000 trades into the future. That's what I want to be focused on."

Tom: Something Van Tharp said a long time ago which I remember so well is, "A good day for a trader is following your strategy." In other words, trying to get to those next 1,000 trades and just doing what you do over and over again. It's not whether you made money or lost money today; it's whether you followed your strategy today and put on that next set of trades that you were supposed to have put on according to your strategy. When you get into that mode, then trading gets a little less exciting. Your stomach lining feels a lot better and you'll have more success.

Michael: You're on Twitter, and you're on Facebook, and you've given a lot of interviews. You stay connected with people and clearly really enjoy it. It's clear from your interviews that you have a definite political opinion. I'm not necessarily curious about the political opinion, because I know what it is, and I share a lot of those beliefs. But I think for some people, they can see the political opinions and get confused.

They can say, "Tom's got this strong opinion," and they could somehow or other think your trading is living and breathing with your political opinion, and it's not.

Tom: Oh, not at all. My political opinion coincides with how I view trading, where traders have to take self-responsibility to be successful. If you're blaming the guys on the floor for screwing you on the trade, or if you're blaming your broker for giving you the wrong advice, you're going to fail. You've got to take self-responsibility and be responsible for pulling the trigger on something. That's what I fail to see a lot throughout political life as well. There's a lot of finger pointing all the time. Something happens and so and so is blaming Congress and Congress is blaming the President and everybody's blaming everybody else.

They're not looking to themselves and asking, "What could I have done?" A lot of my political views come from that same bent, but it certainly doesn't have anything to do with my trading. My trading is just purely mathematical. If the direction's up I want to be long, if it's down I want to be short. It's not any more complicated than that.

Michael: I've interviewed some traders this fall, current CTAs running multi-billion dollar funds, and they'll come on the show and say, "Hey, we're price driven. We're 100% systematic. This is what we do." And I'll get these emails from people saying, "No, you don't get it Covel—there's a secret fundamental overlay; there's discretion going on in the backroom!" It still strikes me as funny that so many trend following traders just like you will come out and say, "This is exactly what we do. There is no fundamental input." And people still think, "No there's a secret sauce of human discretion that you don't know about, Mike, and you're missing the point, and you don't realize that Basso has really got a huge fundamental staff in the backroom."

Tom: I don't have time. I've got to move the five tons of gravel this afternoon. I think it comes down to people loving to have complicated things. A lot of traders, when they start out, what do they do? They go get Covel's book. You get Schwager's stuff, and read, read, read. You get a lot of opinions about all sorts of different ways of trading—fundamental and technical. Then there is the universe type stuff, like Elliott Wave and Fibonacci, and your poor trader starting out just looks at all this and can't figure out what to do next. The human mind wants to make something as important as making money in the markets a very complicated thing. It's almost like people need to think to themselves, "Tom has been around for a lot of years so that's why he's so experienced, and that's why he's successful."

But the reality of it is, simple things work the best. Schwager had a way of saying it: "It's degrees of freedom." In other words, you start out with a simple moving average and say, "I'll only do the buy signal on a moving average if the move is in the right phase," and then you add on that, that you've got to have it only on the open and not any other time during the day, and it's got to meet those criteria. You start adding filter after filter after filter, and pretty soon you won't do a trade. You'll sit there and look at all the stuff and you'll, first of all, be confused because you won't be able to process all that information in your poor brain. Then you'll miss out on trades because you just can't function. There's so much complication by nature.

You sit there and watch the markets, wishing you could trade and make some money. Really, simple things are very robust. There's very little about them that can fail because they're so simple. There's not anything but price. Price feeds your profits, and it feeds your losses, so if you stay to price with all your strategies, you are strategizing on the variable that feeds directly, one to one, to your profits and losses. You never get out of sync.

If you're over there looking at interest rates and trying to predict stock market indices, you've got two different variables going on there. The interest rates may agree with the stock market, or they may not agree with the stock market and we could get caught sideways some place. But if you're looking at stock index prices and you're buying and selling stock indices, it's one to one. You're going to make money or lose money on what stock indices do, and therefore you never get out of whack. You're always in sync with the market and you don't have to stress out on it.

Michael: You mentioned traders having overwhelming amounts of information and confusion with all the different strategies out there, and you mentioned Elliott Wave and Fibonacci. One of the things that I found useful in wrapping my arms around strategies when I was just a new guy trying to understand it all, was not to necessarily just trust what Tom Basso has to say, but I would look at the performance data. Of all the strategies out there in the technical space, I couldn't find any strategy that had this massive number of participants openly putting the performance data out each month where you could compare performance data and see some correlation. I eventually found trend following and said, "Wow, trend following has all these participants that seem to be doing something similar. I feel comfortable about this. This is a useful piece of information for me." Whereas, I've never been able to find that kind of overwhelming amount of data for any other technical strategy. It's only trend following.

Tom: That's correct. You'll find that the trend followers also tend to lose money at the same time. I did studies where I took the average volatility, high-low range of various commodity markets over a month, and then looked at the performance of CTAs in general over that same month. I would find a direct correlation. Highly volatile months led to larger CTA profits, and lower volatility months led to smaller CTA profits or even losses.

It made a lot of sense to me that if people are really trend following, you want the market to go a long way. If it's sitting there in one place, you can't make any money if the prices aren't moving. This is a simple study with a simple result and it leaned exactly the way that I thought it would lean.

It makes sense, doesn't it? If the prices move then trend followers can make some money.

Michael: I'm amazed that so many traders will believe in some type of a strategy, yet they can't find other market participants actually using it. They decide on their lonesome, "I have this one novel strategy," and they must think in their own mind, "It's worth more to me because I'm the only one doing it." Whereas I think, "Hold on. I want to see there's some other smart people before me that have done this."

Tom: That'd be nice. I can't say that trend following is the only way that you could possibly make money in the markets, but it certainly is one that has been tried and tested by a lot of different minds over the years. It's certainly a sound way to approach things and to keep yourself from getting in harm's way too often.

Michael: I have a couple more questions for you and then we'll let you go move some gravel around. While you're doing gravel, I'm going to do yoga. We'll see who sweats more!

People often want to put money with a manager when they've had a great run. It's the human condition. Whereas I think what you showed in a study you did is that reality is a little bit different than what people think.

Tom: I found out that prices move, therefore trend followers make money. Trend followers making money means their equity curve gets better and better, so the trends persist for maybe several months. Maybe the trend followers are now knocking it out of the park, so then all the money in the world starts rushing in. When the market starts stalling out of those trends, the trend followers go sideways or into a drawdown, then at the bottom of a drawdown, at the pit of the trough of the equity curve, markets are now going sideways and are about to break out up or down or whatever. They're just building pressure, waiting for it to explode, and that's when people are pulling money out, just before the next big surge.

I compared the time-weighted return and dollar-weighted return of CTAs. The time-weighted return was what the CTAs will do if you just put your money with them and left it alone. This is the CTAs' returns by strategy. The dollar-weighted return takes into account clients giving the CTAs money at certain times and taking it out at other times.

The time-weighted returns were always better than the dollar-weighted returns. Clients were actually hurting their performance across the entire industry.

Michael: I find it so interesting that so many aspects of successful trend following trading include an understanding of behavioral economics, behavioral finance, and how to deal with biases and using heuristics to trade. Long before it was a popular subject, long before the Nobel Prizes were handed out, there was this group of traders that were essentially trading in a way where clearly they understood all the academic research that was to follow in the decades to come.

Tom: The Turtles.

Michael: Many of your peers. It is fascinating.

Tom: I say if crude oil's going down, it's not up to Tom to figure out how or why it's going down, it's simply going down. Where would you want to be positioned today if you had your choice? Would you rather be enjoying the downside or would you rather be trying to jump in and say, "Low is low, and maybe it's going up from here." To me, if the trend is down, I just want to be short, and when it turns around and goes the other way I want to be long. I don't really want to think too much about it. I've got other things I'd rather think about.

I think that's reacting to the behavior of a whole market full of traders that may or may not be using fundamentals or hedge techniques to make their decisions. The aggregate all feeds into *that* price and makes it go up and makes it go down. So it's the dependent variable of all *that* behavior and decision making of the rest of the market. I'm just reading it in the price and going with it. And I'm not thinking too much more than that about it.

Michael: Life is short and you've got to find ways to enjoy your time and have fun, not sitting around and staring at a screen and talking trading all the time. Trading is a useful by-product of a process of a machine, but I can tell, you don't really care. Trading is not what you are, it's something you know how to do. It doesn't define you.

Tom: I know how to golf, but I don't consider myself necessarily a one-dimensional golfer, and I don't live or die over whether I can get to the golf course. I haven't touched my golf clubs, thanks to the cruise to Tahiti, in about three and a half weeks now. And I'm still enjoying life. It's not like I need to get over there and hit balls right after I get off the phone.

I think a lot of people get into trading and they get addicted to the gambling nature of it all. To me it's just managing my portfolio and the less time I can take to do it, the more time I have to move gravel, or talk to you, or prune my backyard, or go hit golf balls, or take a cruise to Tahiti. A lot of people won't take vacations because they're afraid of missing something in the markets. I just take along my computer and I go do about 10, 20 minutes a day on the ship's satellite internet and I'm done. That's not too burdensome.

Michael: So many people run their lives afraid they will miss something. I think that is what's happened in modern society, especially with the media coverage; it's all built around a really intense fear.

Tom: I think they're going to miss something if they're making decisions based on, "What did the Fed decide today?" They're glued to the screens trying to wait for the Fed's decision to air on TV. I've got to stop sitting there. If the Fed decision causes the market to go through my stop then I can execute it. I find out about it when I close the markets down in the afternoon, which I'll probably do after our call. It's not something I'm going to sit here and wait on until the Fed decides to publish their darn report. That means I'm sitting here all day long in front of a computer? That's not quality of life.

Michael: But Tom, can't you listen to the Fed and use some extra discretion to improve your trend following performance?

Tom: No, I cannot. I cannot, so I just don't. I did enough studies in the early years that talked about the failure of discretionary decision making made in overlaying any trend following. I became clearly convinced that I was not adding any value, so therefore why? I just fired myself basically.

Michael: I love it. It's so fun talking to you because you're so clean, meticulous, and precise about your thinking and about your process, your system, your machine. I just know some people will hear you and they're going to say, "Oh, Tom doesn't know that we can improve what he's doing. It can get better." Almost like *The Six Million Dollar Man*, we can get better, faster, stronger.

Tom: That might be. But we've got to remember I'm 62, retired and enjoying life, so I don't want to create a job out of this. Certainly there're things I can do to try to improve what I'm doing. I'm sure if I had a team of computer programmers like I did back in the old days at TrendStat, I'd probably have a couple of ideas I could work on. But it's just not worth spending that kind of money and effort just to try to pick up a few extra percent here and there. That's not what I do today.

I keep it simple and I keep low fixed overhead with zero regulation fees. I have very little to no chance of somebody suing me, like I did in the old days. You end up with a low liability, easy to run, retirement type of investment strategy, and that fits my situation and my dollars and my expertise level. That's what every trader should always try to get to— examine themselves, their capital and their expertise. Design a strategy around those things, not around what Tom Basso does, or Michael Covel does, or anybody else. Everybody out there needs to do what they need to do for themselves That's what creates the success, because then they can do it over and over again with ease.

If you're trying to copy somebody else, you're not going to ever be at ease with that. You're always going to be trying to compare yourself to *that* person, or trying to do things that are not in your expertise level or maybe you don't have enough capital for. But if you design what you're doing for yourself, then that's where success lies.

Michael: I get emails from young people all the time and they want advice on where they can go to get hired in the CTA space, the trend following space. They ask, "Who will hire me? What insight can you give me?" And I think stories like the Turtle story, for example, have really created the idea that it can be recreated. People think, "I can replicate this if I can just get my toe in the door," whereas I think you have some different perspectives about the managed money space today.

Why don't you talk about that and maybe offer some advice to a young person today that wants to trade. Maybe give an alternate view on ways to go about it versus the ways that people have seen in the last 20, 30, 40 years. You might have a point that things have changed from your perspective, and maybe there's another way to go about it.

Tom: Clearly, if you took today's world, I could not do today what I ended up doing back in the '70s and '80s starting up TrendStat. I don't think that would be a reasonable path to success in today's world. There're too many billion-dollar money managers who have extensive staffs. I have no idea what their criteria are to hire somebody, but I would dare say it'd be hard to get along with a lot of those folks.

And because of the regulation increasing, the cost of doing business is increasing in the CTA space. An easier approach to learning how to trade is to probably become your own trader and continue to work very hard at whatever it is that you did before trading—your main job. Save as much money as you can. Keep building your portfolio bigger and bigger, and keep building your expertise in trading bigger and bigger. At some point you'll be making enough money to look at your trading success and say, "I'm making as much money off of trading as I am being a chemical engineer, for example. Maybe I don't need to be a chemical engineer anymore." Then you transition and then you're where I am right now, trading full-time.

The CTA space has gotten to be very difficult to break into. I'm really at a loss at this point—partly because I've been out of the business for 11 years, but also just because I can't quite see my way clear on how you would go about doing that. You definitely would need capital infusions or partners that would be able to bring in sizeable amounts of assets to trade, to finance a staff of five or 10 at least. Think about all the phone systems, computers, regulatory environment, all the prospectuses—and on some of those prospectuses you can blow $50,000 or $100,000 really quickly with legal expense. It's getting to be a pretty tough game to break into for a little guy operating out of the garage.

Michael: But that doesn't take away from the fact that if you want to trade, trade your money, or your friends' and family's money—that opportunity's wide open. You're not saying trading is tougher to break into, you're saying managed money is tougher.

Tom: The managed money is very tough today and the business of being a CTA is tough. Trading your own money is free of regulation and it's very low overhead. In the old days, having been a manager you could negotiate your commissions and the retail public had to pay a higher brokerage fee. Now everybody pays those brokers' fees. So there's almost no cost to trading these days. You really can, as a small operator, do things that the big guys almost can't do. I'm a small dollar size compared to what I used to be, so I don't have to worry about it. I can go into markets that I didn't go into before very much.

I think you have to examine as an individual trader, "Do you want to go and work as a CTA because you're trying to pick up expertise?" Well, what if their expertise is bad? Say you got a job with John Henry back in the day. He was going up and down with 40% drawdowns. Yeah, he traded billions of dollars. I don't think what he was doing made a super lot of sense to me. I thought it was probably always going to lead to very large drawdowns and runups because he was more leveraged. Maybe if you go work for somebody like that, and he's teaching you that type of trading, you might be learning bad habits.

It's not a panacea to go to work for somebody else and learn what they're doing. I think it's better for you to learn how to do it on your own, and trade your own stuff successfully. Then maybe you arrive right where you need to be. You need to try to find ways of getting more capital to trade and that means working harder, taking a second job, getting maybe a degree to get a promotion, or getting to that next rung up the ladder in the corporate world so that you can have more money to put away.

Michael: I think a lot of people dream and fantasize about the panacea, but there isn't one.

Tom: No, there isn't. Becoming a trader to get to where I am right now, trading my own account, living off it—that is something that is difficult to get to, no matter where you're starting from. Unless you're starting from a major inheritance, and you've got all the money in the world—well that'll be an easier time transitioning. But if you're starting from where I started, as a guy out of college with a $4,000 student loan with a chemical engineering job and zero net worth, or negative net worth actually, I think you have to realize that it's a tough road no matter which way you go.

Tools That Make or Break Us

EPISODE 700: OCTOBER 8, 2018

Michael: As we think about technology, you've told me, "Gosh, $1,000,000 of your own capital to produce computerized trading systems back in the day has come down to roughly a couple thousand dollars now." That brings us to the most important point—the individual. The person.

What is it about the individual and the person that's so important? I know it starts with belief. We need a belief about how things work. Why don't you tell me your thoughts on belief and how some of your most important beliefs have come to be?

Tom: I would say beliefs feed their way into the trading world and even into your living world on the basis that what you believe in becomes your reality. If you believe the markets are rigged, you will find all sorts of excuses to think they're rigged. If you think they're just a bunch of buyers and sellers coming together and price moves around, then you'll just create some trend following models and follow the prices. You won't worry about it beyond that.

If I'm golfing out there, and if I truly believe I will not hit this next shot well, I won't hit the next shot well. When I'm looking at trading strategies and trying to drive down the costs of what I'm doing every day, my belief is that technology is going to keep marching on. Pretty soon the tech that cost $1m in the past is going to be $200. It's just going to get cheaper and cheaper, and faster and faster, and hard drives get bigger. Everything's in the cloud. And you've got servers doing everything. It's an amazing world we live in and I am fascinated by trying to absorb it all. It's a lot of fun.

Michael: The price of technology is coming down and down and down. But that's not everything. I have a mental image right now of walking into a Home Depot. "Okay, I can buy a hammer, but if I buy that hammer, when I put it in my hand it does not build me a house." I need an understanding of *that;* I need a belief of what to do with the hammer to get the value from it.

Tom: That's absolutely true. A lot of studies I did years ago were more of a scientific approach of trying a thesis out, running a bunch of data, trying to simulate it different ways and then figure out, "What did I learn from this?" Then that becomes one more notch in an extensive trading strategy that encompasses everything from buy and sell engines, to position management, to total portfolio management, diversification, portfolio selection and the mental side of trading, then ultimately trying to get all of that to come together to win the day in the end.

I think it's the same way an Olympic athlete is trying to look at every part of nutrition, exercise and mental training to try to become the best they can be. If you take the belief that you can be better than you are today, then you will be better. You'll act on exercise and diet.

I know you're a big fan of yoga and a lot of athletic activity, and you keep yourself in good shape. You can stand on top of your head; I can't. I think that's the type of thing people in the trading world sometimes lose sight of. They're so hung up over the system, the numbers, the buy and sell type engine, that they lose sight of all these other esoteric things that surround that buy/sell engine to make it a really good trading strategy.

Michael: When I listen to you talk, I think, "My gosh, this man has figured out a system, not only for the trading, but a system of self-awareness too." You seem to be very good at looking at yourself in the mirror and not letting the mirror lie to you."

I'm not asking you to be cocky about this, because none of us are perfect, but how have you developed that personal self-awareness system to where there's no excuses, it's all on you, and when you see Tom in the mirror, you're honest with who you see?

Tom: That's a great question. When I was in senior year of high school—I can remember it vividly—I had to do a book report. I was a shy guy. Just completely destroyed. I had no confidence to get up in front of a class of just 20 people, many of whom were close friends, and give a little stupid book report. I'd heard that some people practice speeches in front of a mirror. So I closed the door of the bathroom, I got in front of the mirror, and I started giving a speech. I tried to start making myself look better and it worked. It helped me through getting that speech done, and I survived it.

It became a little bit of an observer self. Then later on as I got into engineering, I was trying to increase my awareness. I read some stories about observer selves where one part of your brain is doing whatever it is that you're doing that day—accounting, working on code in your computer or whatever. That's one part of your brain.

The other part of your brain can be sitting there watching you do that activity. When I found I could do that, I started out doing it by literally putting a little sticky note on my computer. It would say a word of mindfulness, for example, and every time I saw that little sticky tape, I would then stop what I was doing, and make sure my observer self could play back what I had just gotten through. Was I running fast? Was I too slow? Was I not pushing myself enough? Was I allowing myself to become distracted? All sorts of different things. And then I'd go back to work.

Then I'd see the sticky note, and I'd go back into the observer self. It's an exercise and, just like most exercises and habits, little by little you build a habit of doing it more and more, and pretty soon the observer self is there all the time. No more sticky notes.

Then I guess that reached a point where I felt like I was aware of what I'm doing all the time, 24 hours a day. The only time I don't realize what's going on is when I'm, by choice, emotionally involved in a movie or emotionally involved in some activity where I choose to go away from the rational, logical self that I might be more inclined to be when I trade, into an emotional self where I'm enjoying myself. I'm having a good laugh, I'm having a lot of fun, I'm watching a horror flick or a sci-fi flick, and I'm trying to enjoy it.

That was my progression all the way from mirror work, to sticky notes, to having an observer self all the time, and then more into mindfulness.

Michael: You describe a balance between those two different poles in your life—the rational side and the emotional side. You've now been on social media for many, many years, and I know you're not really paid for it, but you've been a big teacher to a lot of people, and a lot of people like to listen to you and observe you. But you must also, just by natural observation of yourself, end up observing other people too. How do you observe balance today when you watch social media? How do you perceive people? Do you perceive a certain part of the population that gets it? A certain part that's striving? A certain part that doesn't get it?

How do you observe so many people on this new platform of connecting with strangers that you've been involved in, my gosh, for the last five, six, seven years?

Tom: It's been fascinating to me that I've been retired from the industry for about 15 years now and I still get four or five emails a day from all around the world. I get messages on Facebook. I've got all sorts of Facebook friends. I've got 8,000+ Twitter followers. I haven't managed any money in 15 years, except for my own, but I've tried to be helpful to everybody who asks a question.

I find it interesting that in terms of social media, so many people are getting so emotional, especially when they're not even friends—I mean true friends. You and I have known each other for some time, so we have a background together. However, some new follower that just came in yesterday, I have no idea who the person is and yet sometimes I'll get critical comments on something I say. They're expressing their own opinion, which is fine with me. I think everybody should be able to express opinions, no matter how insane they seem to be. But what I find happening more in social media is this emotional response to the way that that person believes the world works or the way the government works. They're 100% committed. Very close-minded many times to what other possibilities might be with that situation. It's created this real divisive nature of everything from nutrition, to exercise, to politics. Any topic, you pick it.

I just pulled out an air fryer that I had. It's a little device that you can use to fry without putting stuff in oil, and so I wanted to try it. I signed up for an air fryer webpage in Facebook, and I see all these people that are talking down air friers and there're other people that can't love them enough. It's the same device; how can people be so far apart? They get entrenched. Oh man, it's unbelievable. The sad part of social media is this divisiveness that it seems to bring forth.

If people would open their minds and have discussions and talk through some things with thought-provoking questions and analyze more of the philosophy of the questions and look at both sides, it wouldn't create such divisiveness. Maybe try to argue both sides just to see how you could do it.

Michael: It seems that people have a hard time saying, "This particular side really is to a high degree of probability true. I can accept it, I can use it, I can move on." It seems like a lot of people are in this gray area, because of the fog haze of the consternation of all these people agreeing or disagreeing, and it seems like it's harder and harder for people to make sound decisions.

I think we're a little bit lucky in the sense that we started before the internet, so I still have a very conscious thought process of interaction with people. Real interaction with people. Whereas, for a lot of younger people today, social media is what they know—this faceless idea of people. They might be talking to a real person, perhaps not a real person. This is their life. I don't know if they have the same grounding that you and I might have.

Tom: You're absolutely right. Both of my kids, literally, if I don't message them on the phone, I'm not going to get a response. If I call them, it goes to voicemail. If I send an email, they won't even read it for days. But on social media, if I message them on Facebook or if I message them using a text on the phone, I sometimes get a response by text typed all within 60 seconds. Unbelievable.

They don't talk to people. I've watched my great-niece, who's about 20 years old now and attending ASU, on her phone, complete with nails, go at three times the speed I can go, and she doesn't miss a letter. It's unbelievable.

Michael: I've had Annie Duke on this podcast many times, a professional poker player. In professional poker they have something called TILT, where the player gets into a negative emotional state. They lose track of their system and make bad decisions.

Is there any moment you can really recall of your biggest instance of going on TILT, where you really had to look in the mirror and say, "Man, I know with everything I'm doing right now, this is not right. I need to reassess. I need to stop. I need the stop-loss on me right now. I need to change."

Tom: I remember a very specific example when I was leaving from St. Louis, where we originally had our business. I was doing a business trip to Phoenix, Arizona, where I now live. It was an afternoon flight, TWA out of St. Louis, and I remember living out in the woods southwest of St. Louis. I'm getting ready to leave for the airport, knocking down a couple of cups of fresh coffee, black. I finish off my packing, making sure my briefcase is ready, and I jump in the car.

I head on Highway 44 into the city, then on 270 heading to the airport. I come over the top of a hill and start going down the hill, when I find myself just looking at all the cars around me, and I'm looking for any potential speed traps that might be out there. I realize my fingers are practically white, I am gripping the steering wheel so heavily. I realize that I am going probably 15 or 20 miles over the speed limit.

I realized that all that caffeine had me so jacked up, and I was going to have an hour and a half to kill at the airport before my plane would take off—this is before TSA and all those things. I had put myself in a stressful state for no reason whatsoever, and I realized that the caffeine was clouding my judgment and my awareness of what was happening to me. That same trip to Phoenix, I actually stopped drinking coffee and have been decaffeinated since my 20s now. Occasionally, I might have an iced tea or something, but basically I'm decaffeinated.

That was a real critical awareness thing. I realized I was missing that awareness because I had a chemical in my body that was causing me to speed up, causing my heart to jump a little bit every now and again. It was a profound day. By the time I got back off that trip, I was living in this peaceful world that wouldn't go away, and I've been living in it ever since.

Michael: I would love for you to help me to understand your routine. You've got routines. You've had routines early in life, fund manager routines. You've got certain routines now. Has there been an evolution of routine, or not? Maybe you've been very, very consistent on certain routines. What are those? You just gave one routine—the elimination of coffee. But what are the routines that have worked very well for you for decades?

Tom: A trader has to view himself as an athlete. You can't expect to go out and drink with the boys till midnight or two o'clock in the morning, get a short nap in, and then all of a sudden do a full day in a stressful environment, which trading certainly could be if you let it. Or even when I was running Trendstat: I've got 10 employees; everybody's got questions. They want to know the answer to this and the answer to that or what we should do here and there.

My decisions are going to lead to projects being done timelier, more successfully; or it could be the opposite if I screw it up. So the pressure to perform is always there. I believe that trying to be athletically inclined by clearing your head out and making sure you keep your body fit will help your mind be sharp as well. That's one routine that I've continued all my life.

I always stayed at hotels on the road that had fitness facilities. It was just routine, and I think that's something. Sleep is extremely important as well. I'm 6'3" and as my brother—who's 6'5"—and I were growing like weeds, I think it took a lot out of our bodies growing up. It taught us to rest the body and allow the body to recover because we were growing so fast.

That spilled over into basketball in college, which if you're playing a fast break basketball game, you get done with that, and the adrenalin wears off, and you're pretty much knocked out. You really don't need a lullaby; you're going to sleep really well there.

Then I got out in the real world, where I was doing chemical engineering, starting up a money management business, trying to get an MBA, designing a custom home, taking courses in landscaping and all sorts of things. I didn't have any time to sleep, but when I did have time to sleep I pretty much got my seven to eight hours in, and I was dead to the world. That continued on until we started up the business. I left chemical engineering. Now, I'm traveling the world, I'm jet-lagged every now and again, and I still get a really good night's sleep.

I guess I've been blessed all my life with various conditions that have allowed me to have a good eight hours, sometimes as long as nine hours I'll sleep. I think your brain needs to take those dead brain cells out of there and replace them with some new ones.

I've read a book on neurogenesis, which is the generation of brain cells. They talk about how your brain sort of flushes that old stuff out and brings in the new stuff in deep sleep.

Michael: Let's talk about losing. It's okay to lose, isn't it?

Tom: Yes, I think that losing is especially insightful. Winning a golf tournament, for instance, you really don't know how much better you could have played. But losing, you can go back and remember those two putts that you missed and maybe that one shot that went a little askew. Losing is very educational.

I'm always fond of remembering that famous statement, it might have been from Ed Seykota, which goes: "Trading in an effort to win every time is equivalent to trying to breathe by only breathing in. Breathing out is part of the equation to breathing in, and losing on some trades so that you can win on others is also part of the process." I thought that was brilliant.

Michael: What you just described is hard to internalize, isn't it? If you don't really have the experience or you don't have the mentor that can rigorously bring you into that understanding, it can escape people—escape their understanding.

Tom: Absolutely. In a very top-level, cursory look at losing, say in trading for instance, the new trader will tend to blame himself for that: "I did something wrong, I'm not good enough." Winning a trade means patting yourself on the back, and losing means kicking yourself down and making you less comfortable with yourself—less confident. In reality, I think the experienced trader views the next trade as about the same as his next breath.

It's really not anything; it's just what you do every day. It's the next trade of the next 1,000 trades. You're building this huge database of trades. You know that 35% or something are going to be profitable and 65% are going to be unprofitable, and the average gain is going to be this much, and the average loss is going to be that much. One trade is such an immaterial part of that database that you don't even think about it any more than you'd think about breathing. You just do it.

That's the difference between the new trader and the experienced trader. You start stepping back from the emotional nature of each trade and avoid blaming yourself on the bad side or praising yourself on the good side.

Michael: I caught a tweet recently that was critical of some of my work. It said, "If this guy knew what he was doing, why is he writing books?" And he ended it by saying, "This trend following stuff, this momentum is all chicken bones and tea leaves."

I thought to myself, "I'm the younger guy here who has spent some of his career channeling these people that have come long before me." And then I think to myself, "Okay, let's take Mike Covel out of the equation. Well, that must mean that Tom Basso is into tea leaves and chicken bones too."

Tom: Richard Donchian, back in the day. He was a range breakout trader from before I even came to the industry. What he did back then still would work today, I believe.

Michael: There's a simplicity that is very, very difficult for people to accept. I'd like to throw an association sentence at you—one that I really love, which I think means a lot to you too: "The separation of self-worth from net worth."

Tom: Yes, a very good one. Money does buy certain possibilities and alternatives. It allows you to live in Vietnam if you choose to, or move to the States for the next several months if you feel like doing that. You can't do that for free; it costs some money.

Net worth is useful. But your self-worth, who you are as a person, how you are able to help your family or your friends or your country, that's a whole different animal. They have really very little to do with each other. You really have to separate that out and say, "Net worth is interesting. I like working on that and, sure, I'm not complaining about having an above-average net worth these days. But I don't view that as having anything to do with my self-worth."

I'm more likely to think of my self-worth in terms of helping this golfer I ran into the other day on his putting. He came back, and I saw him last night at a get-together at his house, and he was effusive over how much I helped him and how much it's made a difference in his game. I felt very satisfied that I was able to reach out and help somebody like that. That's more in the area of self-worth, I believe.

Michael: We both know people that have made immense fortunes, perhaps billions of dollars. We also know people that have not made much money. Thinking about that range of possibility, I actually know people that have more self-worth with a net worth less than $100,000. They have more self-worth than some of the guys that I've met over the years that have hundreds of millions of dollars. It's very, very hard for people to accept, that this might be true.

Tom: It's absolutely true. I know people that same way. Sometimes when the $100 million comes in the absence of any other activities that are helping society or helping others, or helping your family, a lot of these people are so driven just to try to get net worth that they aren't thinking through self-worth. They end up cheating themselves and all those around them because they're not doing anything to help the world around them. They're just simply chasing a buck.

They're very shallow people. Many times they have to try to placate their lack of self-worth or self-confidence by buying all sorts of fancy and expensive toys, seven homes, etc. Their lives are miserable because they can never even visit the seven homes they own. They can't drive the 20 cars that they own.

It's just a total waste of time and money, and they would have been better off and probably appreciate their lives more had they taken some of those same dollars and sent them to a charity or maybe started a foundation that awards scholarships to kids trying to get their engineering degree, or something like that. There're lots of things you can do with some of your extra money.

At some point, one of my clients way back had just sold a microwave network for $29 million, and he was a gentleman. I was a young kid and I said, "Boy, I guess you're set for life." And he said, "Son, the first $1 million you make buys you your Cadillac and your home and gives you all the money you need to live the rest of your life. Everything after that is just the score of the game you're playing."

I thought that was in a way very sensibly put, because he sold this microwave network off, and he now is going to do what? He's going to maybe start fooling around with another one. He's not doing it because he's obsessed with dollars; he's doing it because he's intrigued by the puzzle of getting these things to connect to each other, and to him it's just a brain tease, and that keeps him very grounded.

He was a great family man. His wife was sitting there with him. You could tell they loved each other. He was living on a ranch on top of a hill in California; it was really beautiful. You can tell he just relaxes and enjoys life, and it doesn't make any difference whether he's worth $29 million or $1 million or $100 million. I absolutely believe he'd be the same comfortable, confident gentleman.

Michael: If I can be lucky enough to get to the age of 100, health permitting and all that kind of fun stuff, there's a certain attitude I want to convey. I want to be able to talk to someone over the phone when I'm 100 years of age, and them not know how old I am. I think you're one of those guys that's going to be able to pull that off, and I think you know what I'm talking about.

It's the attitude, right? How do you stay young in your energy?

Tom: It's giving myself challenges all the time. I keep coming back to golf. I just played in the senior club championship. I'm 66, and I'm probably one of the more fit guys in my age group because I work out so much, and I keep working on my swing. Well, I tied for the lead after the second day, and we ended up having to go to a sudden death play-off. The sudden death play-off I lost, four shots for him, five shots for me, and one of my putts just went off the edge of the cup.

That type of thing sets a goal for next year that I'm going to win by three, four or five shots. Next year I will attempt to make it not even close. It gives me something to shoot for and it builds the energy. I attack it different ways by saying, "Okay, let's examine my putting; let's examine my full swing. What can I do to shore this up? My mental side? Is there anything I can do to get my mental side more in a steady state while I'm out on the course?"

Those are the types of things that make you young. Trading is the same. I'm still doing research on trading. I'm still helping other people that email me or send me messages on Facebook. They're all around the world. There have been some that I've had to translate from Japanese and Chinese into English so that I can then write the answer and retranslate it back into Chinese or Japanese, but all of a sudden I'm communicating with someone.

There's so much satisfaction in that and it makes you want to get up each morning and say, "I wonder what new brilliant things are going to happen today?"

Michael: I'm not a golfer, but I do like to occasionally observe the majors. I did see the last nine holes of the 2018 PGA Championship. What would be your observation of the mental constitution of Brooks Koepka to pull that out with Tiger chasing him? That was pretty amazing, wasn't it?

Tom: It was. But here's a guy who that morning reportedly was bench pressing 210 pounds, the morning of the last day of that tournament. Now, I don't know about your strength, but I'm not going to be bench pressing 210 on my best day ever.

When you have that kind of strength, and you know that you've got that kind of strength, and you know you can hit that ball 320, 340 yards just on command, and you know you're feeling strong, you're feeling like you're ahead in the lead. You're looking over at Tiger Woods and saying, "He was good once but he doesn't bench press 210 pounds. I've got everything in place that I need to do to win this thing, and I'm going to go do it." Ignore the guy trying to make the comeback who may be a bit past his prime; certainly his back is past its prime.

I mean, Tiger's strong; he works out a lot. I'm just not sure that the way he is working out—or even Brooks Koepka, for that matter—is conducive to better golf. It does make you strong mentally, because somebody that puts their body through that and realizes they can do it, I think they've shored up their mentality too. It does take a mental side to train at that level of sport, and to keep it up, be disciplined about it and push yourself. Certainly Brooks has done that. Tiger's done it too.

I'm amazed Tiger's even playing golf after all the surgery he's had on his back, and yet he's playing it at a top 50 golfer in the world level. Good for him.

Michael: I remember the measurement for the NFL draft combine when I was aged 19. They would see how many times you could bench press 225 pounds. At one weird point in my life when I was lifting a lot of weights, I did that 12 times once. When I read about Brooks Koepka, he actually did it 14 times at his age that morning. 225 pounds, 14 times before the final round of a major. Everyone's got their own way of getting to a place of mental strength, but that really truly is remarkable. I'm sure that's never happened before in golf.

Tom: I'd be very surprised, too. That's a lot of weight. I mean, that's more than I weigh. That's lifting Tom Basso over your head or up off your bench. It is an amazing amount of weight. Not surprisingly, that shaft that he swings is bending like crazy as he's coming into the ball, and it's just pounding the ball out there.

There's a lot of mental side that goes into training at any level. That bleeds into mental strength, as when you face adversity on the course you draw upon that inner strength and say, "No, I've got this. I'm strong, I can hit this next shot well. Let's do it, and let it go."

Michael: Word association for you: "Life is the dancer and you are the dance."

Tom: That's interesting. That's saying that life is the lead and imposing its whims on you—then you have to dance with that in mind. That's what I would associate with that. Another one that's just like that: "You can't change the direction of the wind, but you can change your sails."

Michael: Trend Following 101.

Tom: Exactly. It's Trend Following 101. If the market wants to go down 50% from here, it's going to do it. All you can do is react to it and position yourself appropriately. Change the sails.

Michael: That's one of the things that's hard for people to understand about trend following. You just mentioned the market could go down 50% from here. That doesn't mean you wake up tomorrow and start taking an action based on your belief that the market will go down 50%, but you are prepared for whatever may happen.

Tom: Yeah, it might go up 100% over the next year, starting tomorrow. It might go down 50%. I'm prepared for both. I'd probably do better financially if it went up, but I'm fully prepared to put on the hedges, to batten down the hatches, to sell out of a few stocks and to deal with futures trading. I have systems and strategies in place to deal with what could happen no matter which way it goes.

If you've done a good job of planning your investment strategy, then I believe you should have looked at up markets, down markets, and sideways markets and know what's going to happen with all of them, and be prepared for that.

Michael: You should know what's going to happen with your action, your decision making, based on what the market does?

Tom: Correct. If I'm a trend follower, for instance, and I'm trading gold, and gold starts moving upward, it's going to sooner or later kick off some indicators that say the trend is now up, so you buy it. You put a stop behind it, and then you allow it to keep going and you follow the trend.

When it starts running out of gas and turning around and changing the direction to down, you go ahead and take your profits, hopefully. Or, if you don't have a profit, you take a loss, and you're out and going the other way maybe. You're not anticipating anything, you're just reacting to what the market's doing.

Michael: I don't necessarily have questions when I talk to you. I put it out there, and what I love is that you just react. There's a whole other lesson that people can take from life—whatever's thrown at you, ponder, think, respond, give a good reaction. That in itself is a great lesson you're giving people. How does one manage a conversation, how does one manage interactions with people? I think you're exceptional at that.

Tom: Perhaps. I guess part of that ability is, of course, living a life around the world, as you and I both have done, and dealing with a wide variety of markets over a wide range of years—up markets, down markets, sideways markets. Dealing with answering three to five emails or messages a day from various traders asking questions, you get to the point where you know the material so well. I know how my life has gone. I've been very introspective about how I've had to deal with life in general, whether it be nutrition, exercise, family issues, or whatever it may be.

That allows me, at my more advanced age than you, to be able to hear a question. Chances are I've already thought about the question or I've been asked about it before. Do you know what I mean? It's like I'm speaking from a vast quantity of experience, so that when you give me an association question, it's pretty easy for me to think through my life real briefly and come up with an answer off the top of my head because I know the topic.

Michael: I remember asking Leo Melamed of the Merc (CME) a question when I interviewed him. His first response was, "How did you know to ask me that question?" I said, "I read your book."

That's the fun part of doing an interview: Trying to find places where a guy like you, Tom, might not yet have ventured to. That's the challenge of doing an interview.

Tom: Right. You are always well prepared for these interviews compared to other interviewers that I've had in my past. I think when you ask a question that gets into the self, that gets into my mind, and how I dealt with issues, those are the most fascinating things to a lot of people. They're going to face those same issues a lot of times in their life, and maybe they aren't even aware that they've got those issues. Maybe we get them to start thinking, "How am I dealing with stress in the markets?"

My view of stress would be that there're potential stressors out there, and if you accept them into your life and you allow them to change you, then they become stress. But to me stress is you allowing stress to happen.

Think of a guy that diffuses bombs. He's down to 10 minutes, and he's got to find the right wire to cut. That's a lot of potential stress, but if you could somehow magically just be cool, collected, trace the wires and figure out which one to cut, the bomb's diffused and you're safe.

That's where a lot of these mental things come in. Some people, including on social media that you talked about, are so into a very shallow level of thinking when it comes to the way their life is. They don't look introspectively into how they're affecting other people around them or how they're even affecting themselves over the long run. They are creating extra stress for themselves that's unnecessary. Creating a lot of illusions around themselves that their life is not very real. It's sad we've come to that. I'm with you; I love to sit down and just talk to somebody. It's very refreshing.

Michael: How does one find meaning? For example, I have noticed young men and women of all ages—20s, 30s, 40s—using social media as a way to try to present an image of themselves. So much of it is not real.

I have a 13-year-old niece, and I really wonder about how one finds meaning as a young person when they're bombarded with so much social media stuff that's inconsequential.

But then, I don't know if you're aware of this, the youngest Kardashian, 21 years of age, is about to become the youngest self-made billionaire in America—about to beat out Zuckerberg—because she started a cosmetics line. So you and I can lament some of the negatives of social media, but then the young people can say, "Well, what about the youngest Kardashian? She's made $1 billion off her cosmetics' empire, and it's all based on Instagram photos." It's a really interesting conundrum, isn't it?

Tom: It is. I'm all for people being entrepreneurial and doing whatever they can. If she is using social media as a platform to build sales in her products, and that has got her to where she was trying to get to with her business, I'm a big fan.

If it's one of my young relatives, just trying to project an image to get their next 1,000 followers, then I'd say, "What's your goal here? What's the end gain? So you're going to have 2,000 friends and you're going to have a bunch of people tracking you. Where does that lead? What's the logic and what's the end gain here?" Most people don't seem to think through the long term.

The trading world is not immune from this. I see new traders starting up, and they fancy themselves maybe as money managers someday, but they don't have enough track record yet to sell and get registered. You can see them trying to pump up the idea that they caught cryptocurrency at the right time, or they did this and that. They're trying to build a following and get more friends and show their charts and talk about their successes. What's the end gain of that? You're not going to get anywhere.

Your following is going to be based on you pumping yourself up, but if you end up getting into the business and you don't have the substance behind it, you're just going to have a hard fall. I don't think people think through their own lives strategically. For example, Snapchat messages disappear after how many minutes or seconds? Crazy stuff. Forcing you to have to stay connected to what the other person in the conversation is saying right now.

You have to drop everything, go to your phone, and look at what they say. If you don't, it's going to disappear. It's unbelievable how that warps your life and makes it very shallow.

Michael: I look at these things as again like the trading software or the hammer. These are just tools. If we can keep them in our mind as tools, things to advance our life in a positive way, that's great. But if the tool owns us, we're in trouble.

Tom: Right, exactly.

PART II

Collected Research and Publications

The following chapters present a series of research reports and publications by Tom Basso, as well as Tom's podcast interview with Aaron Fifield on *Chat With Traders*.

Adding Low Sharpe Ratio Investments Can Increase Your Sharpe Ratio

MANY fund of funds managers have focused their attention on higher Sharpe ratio managers with as little correlation as possible. The logic is by adding many high Sharpe ratio managers together you get an even higher Sharpe ratio portfolio.

By comparison, CTA style hedge fund managers have had lower Sharpe ratios than the traditional hedged managers.

Some fund of funds have ignored this area because of the lower Sharpe ratios. This study shows that to be an oversight on their part, since adding lower Sharpe ratios actually increased the Sharpe ratio of the total fund.

Background on the study

To obtain proxies for both the fund of funds and the CTAs I used MAR's fund of funds median (FOF) and the Trader Advisor Qualified Index (CTA) going back to January of 1990. I used the monthly median numbers for the FOF group and the monthly averages for the CTA group.

Next, I combined the returns together in various combinations from 0% CTAs all the way to 100% CTAs. The 0% level is the level some fund of funds currently allocate to CTAs. The 100% level is where some commodity pool operators operate their pools, not using hedge funds in the portfolio. I also tested a variety of other combinations in between these two extremes.

To calculate a reasonable Sharpe ratio, I used a 4% risk-free rate over the period. I used the annualized returns of the portfolios, minus 4%, divided by the monthly standard deviation of the returns.

Figure A: Sharpe ratio with addition of various % CTAs in a fund of funds

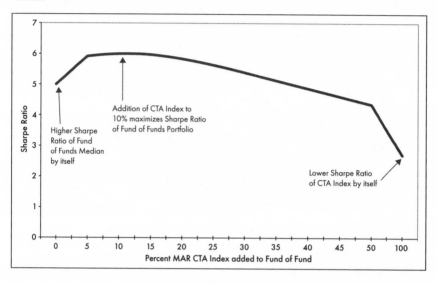

Results of the study

In Figure A, I plotted the amount of the CTA investment in the fund of funds index against the Sharpe ratio for each combination. The Sharpe ratios were higher with the addition of some CTA index to the FOF index. High Sharpe ratios were found between 5%–15% of the total portfolio. The highest Sharpe ratio was achieved by adding 10% CTAs to the FOF portfolio.

Using the research

In the study I used indices for fund of funds and CTAs. Because of that, my numbers are already going to be smoothed and Sharpe ratios higher than they might be on average for individual managers. Fund of funds attempting to add CTAs can look at extremely diversified CTAs that would correlate well with MAR's CTA index, hire several CTAs that use different strategies, or use an indexed approach to adding a CTA style return/risk component to their portfolios.

Algorithmic Trading Is Getting a Bad Rap

WE'VE heard it every time the stock market takes a serious hit. "Those Algos are at it again," or "Algos are bad because they are creating more volatility in the markets."

Any time any of us creates a strategy in Excel, Trading Blox, or similar platforms, you become an Algo. You are simply taking your own inventory of yourself (capital, skills, resources, available time) and creating something you hope will lead to what you deem success. I have 50+ years of trading experience, computer skills, math skills and am retired. My measure of success is to trade for capital preservation while increasing the value of my assets. Sleeping at night is important to me.

Others might opt for more leverage and "action" with larger overall profits. Still others might shoot for more reliability, looking to be more right than wrong in trade success. Some might like to trade with the trend, others might fade the trend. There's something for every taste and style here in the world of trading.

Algorithms are nothing more than the mathematical representation of the opinions and desires of the person creating the algorithm. I do agree that Algos have helped the market move more quickly, but I don't believe that is due to the algorithm as much as it is the more efficient execution of the algorithm designers' opinions and biases.

When I started automating my strategies back in the Trendstat days, I was proud to have a very new IBM PC in 1980 that was more powerful than anything I could get my hands on before. Today my phone has more RAM and computing capabilities. I'm now running a laptop that fits in my backpack for traveling that has 64 gigabytes of RAM, a quad processor and 2 tetra bytes of disk storage for $2,800!

Let's go back in the time machine and look at what was happening when I graduated from Clarkson University back in 1974 as a chemical engineer. That was the end of a two-year bear market. Stocks had fallen by roughly 50% from the highs. *The Wall Street Journal* was printing opinions about how far the market had to go down to reach the bottom. When the New York Stock Exchange had more than 10 million shares traded, they broke out the champagne. Fast forward to 2018 and the Standard & Poor's 500 Index (S&P 500) exchange traded fund (ETF), ticker SPY, routinely trades 200 million plus shares in a day! This single ticker can easily trade more than 20 times the amount traded on the entire NYSE back in 1974!

So is it the algorithm that is causing it, or the fact that in every part of our life computers and fast communications have allowed the world to move faster? In 1974, it took two years to beat up investors enough with a bear market to cause them to adopt the attitude: "Stocks are risky, and I'm never going to get into them again." Nowadays, computers allow the market to move so fast that the same amount of pain can be inflicted more quickly with a similar attitude being adopted by those who didn't manage their risk well. And the other side of it, something you'll never hear the public complain about, is the Algos make the up markets happen more quickly as well. Do the Algos get credit during bull markets?

Nothing has changed with the psychology of the situation. Traders will still be traders. There will still be excessive optimism at market tops and excessive angst at market bottoms and trading will go on. Algorithms and the traders running them are simply getting a bad rap.

Currency Investing— Increasing Net Worth While Protecting Net Wealth

EVERYONE's invested in currencies, yet some don't know it.

As I travel the world to conferences, client meetings and vacations, I am constantly running into people who are interested in investing in one form or another. It doesn't matter whether the individual has a lot of money or a little, is in Europe or the States, is investing for a corporation or for himself. If they find out that I'm a money manager, the topic of conversation shifts to investments.

Invariably, I mention somewhere along the way that I trade a fair amount of currencies. The usual reaction: "Wow! That's pretty risky, isn't it?" My answer: "It depends on how you decide to invest and how much leverage you put into the portfolio—and by the way, you're already invested in currencies."

Every investor everywhere is investing in currencies, whether he likes it or not. His portfolio could be in stocks, bonds, futures or real estate, but whatever he owns, it's denominated in some currency, and like it or not, that currency is fluctuating over time. One might say that every investment has at least two components: the actual investment itself and the currency the investment is denominated in. Most investors concentrate on the former and ignore (or are ignorant of) the latter.

Net Worth versus Net Wealth

I like to think of it as a Net Worth versus Net Wealth challenge. An investor's Net Worth is simply his assets minus his liabilities. It's usually denominated in some home currency. That investor's Net Wealth is the amount of goods and services he can buy across the world with his Net Worth. If a stock portfolio increases, while the investor's home currency falls by a similar amount, Net Worth increases, while Net Wealth remains unchanged. That does little to advance the investor's financial condition.

My biggest concern, as a US investor, is the possibility of the stock and bond markets of the world and the US dollar all falling at the same time. Most US investors would have few places to hide, and they would surely watch both their Net Worth and their Net Wealth plummet. They would find themselves with a seriously declining standard of living. Protecting stock and bond portfolios is not the focus here, but protecting the value of the portfolio's currency value is something currency traders routinely attempt to achieve.

The industry has around 60 speculative currency trading programs of any size and there are all sorts of currency overlay programs to hedge the currency exposure of investor portfolios. Investing a portion of a diversified portfolio into a speculative currency portfolio would be one way to gain some protection against major currency swings. Presumably, a major move down in your home country's currency would produce potential profitable trading opportunities for the currency trading program to offset some of the loss of purchasing power in the portfolio.

Another way to attack the risk would be the use of a currency overlay program on the portfolio. Here, a portion of the portfolio is used as margin to cover positions in the currency markets that should reduce the risk of currency fluctuations. This can be done on a passive, active or speculative basis. The first two are traditional and usually cost the portfolio some return to put in place. They both involve taking positions against the negative move of the investor's home currency. The speculative approach is my favorite and attempts to hedge the portfolio, while providing a slightly positive return over time. Here, a speculative trend following program is structured to a size roughly approximating the risk of the portfolio to be hedged. This yields a speculative program, attempting to produce a profit, but inversely correlated to the underlying portfolio's currency risk when it needs to be inversely correlated to it.

Reasonable goals here should be to tie up perhaps 5% or less of a portfolio, produce a 0%–6% increase in the portfolio's returns per year over time, and cost the portfolio no more than about 2%–4% in potential drawdowns. It is difficult to use the inter-bank markets for anything less than about a $25 million portfolio, due to the sizes of trades in that venue. Under that level, you probably should consider a currency program based in the futures arena.

Currency values—the score of the game we're all playing

When it comes right down to it, the value of a country's currency doesn't have a true inherent value. It's just the score of the game each country is playing to be the best country out there. Fundamental traders would cite GDP growth rates, interest rates and economic conditions as determinants of currency value. Opportunistic traders might say political events and announcements drive the values of one currency against another. Technical traders might simply buy the breakouts or measure the momentum of the markets.

In the end, it's all of these things. It's the score of one of the most complicated games in the world. How one country fares in getting the value of its currency to go higher is dependent on political, economic, interest rate factors and the perception, by the currency trading community, of how well one country appears as a place to park one's assets versus another country. Perhaps we should pay our countries' leaders like we pay most currency traders: part management fee, part incentive fee based on how well the leader's home currency fares against a basket of other currencies. That would truly link our leaders' economic incentive to the citizens' macro-economic well-being.

Good Trading Is Not
Rocket Science

ARE successful traders smarter than unsuccessful traders because they seem to be able to produce profits where others fail? Are smarter traders more able to discover the secret keys to success in trading? Although many struggling traders may believe successful traders are smarter, I know of no evidence to support this theory.

Actually, there have been a number of recent examples of just the opposite: huge losses created by very smart people. In a *SmartMoney* article by Eleanor Laise, entitled "If We're So Smart, Why Aren't We Rich?" (June 2001), the author tells of a MENSA investment club, with very high IQ members that produced extremely low returns of +2.5% over the last 15 years in stock investments. Over that same period, the world saw record moves in stocks across the globe.

Long-Term Capital had its share of brilliant Nobel Laureates on the board when it leveraged itself into a financial debacle that rocked the stock and bond markets in August of 1998. Losses were so large that a number of the larger prime brokers had to step in to unwind the firm's positions and cover some of the losses to help protect the integrity of the financial markets.

Michael Berger, a central figure in the Manhattan Fund debacle—where investors lost over $400 million due to ill-fated short-sale strategies in a bull market—has been described as extremely knowledgeable, capable and very believable. It took a lot of brilliant thinking to hide these massive losses from investors for as long as he did.

So why do so many intelligent traders lose money in the markets? In my 25 years in the trading business, I've seen many very smart people struggle to produce a bottom line. Some of the mistakes that these traders tend to make are:

1. **Not diversifying because they know they're right.** Smart people know they're smart. They've made good grades all their life and maybe collected a few scholarships along the way. They've got multiple degrees. They can recall obscure pieces of information on many topics. People tell them they're smart. All of this can go to their head, if they're not careful. Eventually, they get taught a lesson that they cannot outsmart the market.

2. **Not using a sell strategy.** Smart people know they've stacked the odds in their favor and have done their homework. They don't believe they can fail. Maybe they've never failed at anything significant before in their lives. Who needs a sell strategy when you know you're right? The market has ways of teaching these people a lesson.

3. **Averaging down in a losing position.** It the investment idea was good before, it's an even better deal now, because they can buy it cheaper. The market can continue lower, beating them up severely and sometimes putting them out of the game.

4. **Thinking that exhaustive, long-term studies of a strategy can predict the future.** Like the disclaimer always says, historical results do not give an indication of future profits. This is actually true and backed up by countless studies of traders across lots of markets, across lots of strategies and across lots of time periods. Smart people sometimes think that, by taking vast sums of data and analyzing it to death, they have an edge in predicting what the market will do next. Blowups can and will occur when the market does something it has never done before.

5. **Over-optimizing a strategy using historical data.** Since smart traders have the mental ability to think up all sorts of ways of trading, they can come up with countless parameter sets in their strategies to trade a historical database with wonderful results. The problem generally becomes that they are fighting the last battle with the markets in their simulations, not necessarily the next one that they should be concentrating on. They don't give themselves what-if scenarios that might occur and prepare for them properly.

6. **Searching for perfection.** Intelligent traders can come up with so many better ways to potentially trade, they sometimes spend most of their life searching for perfection, rather than trading the best strategy they have at the moment and realizing they can work at making it better over the long run. You'll never have the perfect trading strategy. Just give it the best shot you can each day, and never stop trying to make it better.

7. **Frequently changing an existing losing trading strategy to a "better" strategy.** Smart people may have very active minds that can dream up all sorts of new, "better" ways to trade. Some of these methods of trading can even be very complicated, to satisfy their intellectual firepower. But if you make the assumption that all strategies have their day in the sun and their day in the doghouse, then moving away from a losing strategy may be very foolish. The strategy that looks hot right now may become very cold down the road and this year's mediocre strategy may become next year's star performer.

Now that we've discussed how some very intelligent traders fail to make a passing grade at trading school, here are a dozen common-sense things that successful traders do to be successful at their craft:

1. **Create and understand the strategy you intend to use in your trading.** If you don't understand why you are doing what you are doing, how can you expect to keep doing it? Buying a black box system of some sort, that advertises some profits, is not going to give you the comfort level to stick out a tough drawdown when the markets aren't cooperating with your strategy. Knowing what went into your strategy and why you expect some losses will give you that psychological stomach lining to stay the course on your strategy and enjoy the next period of profitable trading.

2. **Match your strategy to your personality, ability, skills, time commitment and capital to be invested.** Sit down and do an inventory of these things and frequently you'll be well on the way to the approach you should take toward trading. If you're not a computer expert, you may find you either need to develop a strategy that doesn't involve computers or take some computer courses to improve your skill levels in that area. It makes no sense whatsoever to try to trade the way

someone else trades. They have their own skill level, abilities, resources and you have yours. By using someone else's trading strategy, you'll be underutilizing some of your skills and resources and be in over your head on others. Actually, I have known some potential traders that have taken a serious inventory of their trading resources and skill and decided they should not be a trader. That's okay.

3. **Eliminate any notion that profits equal good trading.** Good trading is following your strategy and managing your risks. When you are in the act of trading, simply execute the strategic plan. If you executed the plan and took loses that day, you get kudos for your efforts. Executing the plan over the long run will create the profits, not the efforts of a single trade or a single day's trading.

4. **Diversify your portfolio.** Having a concentration in one market or position can be extremely profitable, but it can also knock you out of the game. It's common sense to not put yourself in a position where you cannot come back tomorrow and continue your trading. Spreading your risks is a simple way to help reduce the impact of a serious loss of capital.

5. **Concentrate your portfolio.** This suggestion would seem to be at odds with the last suggestion, but it means getting your portfolio down to a size where it can be effective without over-diversifying it. Many professional traders, with all the computer firepower, have taken to trading hundreds of markets, only to find that a handful of markets create the bulk of their profits. Trading in markets that fit your strategy or that you have an expertise in makes more sense than mindlessly diversifying beyond what you can logically handle.

6. **Watch your leverage.** The more brilliant a trading strategy seems to be, the more the expectation of profits lures traders to leverage it up. After all, why just make X%, when you can make X% times 2 or 3? The answer is that you want to be there tomorrow trading and too much leverage can knock you out of the game, if a few positions go against you. Dial in your trading leverage so that you can tolerate the amount of risk you are taking on and you can make a career of trading.

7. **Take the attitude that gains AND loses are part of the deal.** You can't have one without some of the other. Understand that every strategy will have periods where it absolutely nails the markets and creates nice profits. However, every strategy has its Achilles heel and will struggle

at times. This is simple common sense—and yet, how many times do we see investors and traders abandon a trading strategy after a string of losses? Did they really expect to not have some losses?

8. **Make your own decisions on trading.** Believe it or not, a simple, unsophisticated trading decision by you is far better for your trading success than trading a tip from some analyst or industry guru, because you will understand why you did it and can control the risk on the trade according to your strategy (see number 1). You don't know what went on in the analyst's head when doing the analysis. You don't know what their tolerance of risk is. You might not know whether or not they've got a position in the recommendation. You might not know where or when they will exit the trade. Making your own decisions on trading empowers you to have control of your trading strategy and risk management.

9. **Let gains run and cut losses short.** Repeated often in articles like this, but not followed by those who "know" they are smarter than the markets. No matter what the strategy, you have to buy low, sell high, or sell high, buy low in order to produce a profit. I maintain that even spread traders and arb traders are taking a position in the spread or the arb. So, no matter what the strategy, if you don't cut losses short, your account could get severely damaged sometime down the road.

10. **Know where you are getting out of a trade before you get in.** Many investments are "sold" to the client. Some traders get into this same mentality. They think of all the reasons they want to own a position in something, but forget that somewhere along the way they'll need to be out of that position. I recommend setting strategy upfront on conditions necessary for you to get out of the position. This could include cutting losses short at some level or taking profits after a trailing stop level is breached. If you don't have an exit strategy, don't put the trade on.

11. **Treat each trade like it's the next trade in a sample of the next 1,000 trades.** It's not life or death. It's just another trade. It may seem important at the time, but it's just another data point in the sample of the trades you'll do over your lifetime. Don't make it any more important than that.

12. **If it ain't broke, don't fix it.** So many traders jump from strategy to strategy, never sticking with anything very long. Historical simulations can be useful in helping the trader gain a feel for the volatility of a strategy or some of the ways the strategy reacts to various conditions in the market. All strategies will have periods of lackluster or even losing performance. If this is extraordinarily different from what was expected, it's time to dig in and determine why. However, if the losses are well within what you should have expected when you started trading the strategy, then suck it up and stay the course.

You don't have to be a brilliant genius to be a good trader. There certainly have been a lot of smart people over the years that have lost vast sums of money. At the same time, there have been many traders that do not have intellectual pedigrees that have made huge profits. All of the suggestions I listed above are things that any trader serious about trading successfully could handle. If you do happen to have the burden of a brilliant mind, be smart enough to realize high IQ does not correlate with large trading profits. Trading success comes from sound strategies, excellent risk control, strict discipline and a good dose of common sense.

Some Leverage Is Good, Too Much Is Dangerous

Purpose of the study

AFTER the Long-Term Capital debacle in August and September of 1998, investors are appropriately more concerned with the use of leverage by hedge fund managers. If leverage is being used and the fund lacks transparency, clients are faced with the prospect of not knowing what the positions are and how much those positions are leveraged.

Some clients trying to cut down the potential misuse of leverage try to set some level of leverage that makes sense. For instance, a long/short manager could be long 100% of his portfolio and short 100% of his portfolio, leading to a 2-to-1 leverage. An event-driven manager may be out of the market for a while, then in leveraged 5-to-1 on a special situation. An arb manager may need 10-to-1 leverage to make the returns interesting to the investor.

Defining leverage

The first problem facing investors is a lack of consistency in what managers call leverage. For instance, a long only stock manager, buying everything for cash, might claim he's at 1-to-1 leverage. Another manager trading cash currencies might claim to be 1-to-1, since he's borrowed no money to put on some positions. However, the currency position's face value may be up to 25 times the leverage of the required good-faith deposits on the trades.

The easiest way to compare a market or strategy to another is to define leverage as the face market value of all the investments in the portfolio to the equity in the account. This puts all investments on a equal definition footing for comparisons.

Leverage varies by markets

Markets tend to move at very different speeds. In Table A, I compiled the history of a number of different markets with daily data from January 1, 1990 until the end of February 1999. The average volatility of a market was calculated using the absolute value of the percent price change each day. The standard deviation of the daily volatilities was also calculated using the daily data. Since the stock market is represented in so many portfolios, I used the S&P 500 Index as the benchmark against which the other markets would be measured.

Table A: Leverage needed to match volatilities in various markets

Market	Average daily volatility	Standard deviation of daily volatility	Leverage required to equal S&P 500 at 2/1
S&P 500 Index	0.6298	1.0323	2.0000
SL-Bond Index	0.4020	0.3757	3.1303
Japanese Yen	0.5303	0.5450	2.3754
Crude Oil	1.3964	1.5800	0.9021
Live Cattle	0.5931	0.5166	2.1239
Gold	0.4859	0.5562	2.5924
Total all non-S&P markets	0.6815	0.7147	2.2254

As you can see from Table A, all the markets listed exhibit less volatility than the S&P 500 Index, except for crude oil, which had some wild swings during the Gulf War.

Good use of leverage

A good use of leverage is to lever markets with less movement in order to match volatilities across a portfolio. For instance, if we were to match volatilities in the portfolio of markets shown in Table A, we would have to leverage the non-S&P markets by about 2.22-to-1 in order to bring them into balance so that none of the markets dominated the portfolio. This would be a prudent use of leverage, designed to balance the portfolio's diversification.

Leverage varies with strategy

Various strategies require extra leverage to make them interesting to investors. In Long-Term Capital's case, one might argue they went too far in levering their fixed income arbitrage bets, but nobody would argue that they should use no leverage in their strategies. The returns would be so low and stable they would struggle to compete with bank CDs (certificates of deposit).

I looked at the leverage numbers in MAR-Hedge's Performance Evaluation Directory for the first half of 1998. The first thing I noticed was that the numbers offered by the managers are inconsistent, but it was the only information I could obtain in the public domain. I broke the leverage numbers down into various logical ranges. I decided that most long-only and long/short managers would tend to fall into less than 2-to-1 leverage, so that was my first range. Next came many of the Global Macro and CTAs in the 2-to-3 range. Finally, I measured greater than 3 and up to 5, followed by all those over 5. I also kept track of the group of managers that either couldn't or wouldn't answer the question, a group that might cause investors some concern of the unknown. The results are shown in Table B.

Table B: Percentage breakdown of various leverage levels in hedge fund industry

Leverage range	Number of funds	Percentage of funds
Less than 2	616	68.8
2 to 3	138	15.4
3 to 5	46	5.1
Greater than 5	60	6.7
Unknown	35	3.9
Total of all funds	895	100.0

Most of the funds (68.8%) fall into the less than 2 range. However, 31.2% of the funds are more levered than 2-to-1. This doesn't mean they are too leveraged. It is very inappropriate to say that the managers at 5-to-1 are uniformly more dangerous than those at 2-to-1.

Where leverage becomes dangerous

Where does the leverage that the manager uses become dangerous? It varies with each strategy used by the manager. Using Trendstat as an example, I can say that our mutual fund timing and allocation programs are 1-to-1 leverage. Our World Currency program runs about 2.7 on average, below average for currency traders. Our FX Extra is closer to 5, much more in line with other currency traders. Our Multi-trend program is over 3, within norms for that investment area and strategy.

The point I'm making is that it isn't the leverage number that by itself makes something dangerous. I don't view our World Currency at 2.7 times leverage as more dangerous than our Sector Allocation program at 1-to-1. They are actually quite similar in the speed at which they move on a given day. Sometimes the currency program moves a little quicker, sometimes the Sector Allocation program is the fastest of the pair.

The investor needs to find leverage figures of comparable managers, before making any rash decisions that leverage is too high or not high enough. When a manager is more highly levered than others with similar strategies, investors should be wary of the additional leverage risk.

Study of Time Spent in Trending and Sideways Markets

Purpose of the study

INVESTORS who time the stock market are constantly faced with the prospect of becoming impatient when, over a shorter time frame, there doesn't seem to be value added by a timing strategy. Frequently, their excuse for abandoning a timing strategy is "it doesn't work anymore" or "I could have made more money with a buy and hold strategy."

Investor psychology is heavily at work here. The investor, at that point, does not remember why they developed or started using their timing strategy in the first place. Many times, I have seen investors forget what to expect in the best case, worst case, and expected case scenarios. I maintain that if the investor can understand exactly what to expect from a strategy, they will be less surprised when the timing strategy does exactly as expected. I constructed this study to help investors learn more about the action of the stock market and what timing programs generally should provide the investor.

Markets move up, down and sideways

All markets spend their time moving up, down or sideways. Markets are a supply and demand battle between buyers and sellers. When both buyer and seller are happy with a price, a transaction takes place and a price is established. If the buyers are more aggressive than sellers, then prices will trend upward. If sellers want to sell more than buyers want to buy, prices will be soft and head down. When buyers and sellers are roughly in equilibrium, prices will drift, creating a sideways market.

How to measure the trend of a market

In order to measure the trend of the market, I created two simple exponential moving averages. An exponential moving average uses the general formula of:

Today's Average =
Yesterday's Average + Beta × (Today's Price − Yesterday's Average)
Where:
Beta = 2 / (Number of Days +1)

I used betas of 0.25 and 0.05 or the equivalent of 9 and 41 days respectively. If the shorter-term, faster moving average crossed the longer-term, slower moving average, a directional change was noted. If that change carried more than 5% in that direction, I deemed it a successful trend. If it failed to move at least 5% before the next direction change, I labeled it sideways market action.

The theory of timing in an up stock market

When a market shifts from a "down" to an "up" reading on the indicator, a timing model moves all your cash to a stock-oriented mutual fund. It does not buy at the exact bottom. Actually, the indication of a change of direction happens after the market bottom. This means the model will miss out on a small amount of the up move. As the market moves up, a growth stock fund typically moves up. What the investor should expect during this type of market are large positive returns, but probably a struggle to keep up with a buy and hold strategy.

Timing a down stock market

When a market shifts from an "up" to a "down" reading, a timing model should move your entire portfolio from a growth stock mutual fund to a money market fund. The timing strategy usually will not sell at the exact top. Money market funds are priced at $1.00 per share each day and simply pay the investor interest. With no risk due to stock market fluctuations, money markets become a good place to "ride out the storm" of a down market move. In this type of market, a timing model attempts to produce about a break-even return and at the same time drastically outperform a buy and hold strategy by not taking substantial losses.

Timing a sideways stock market

Timing sounds like a flawless strategy if you read the up and down market sections above. But, unfortunately, there are periods where the timing programs produce negative returns and underperform the market. When the market drifts sideways, the trend indicators can turn up, then down, then up, then down ... This is known as being "whipsawed."

Each time the strategy gets an "up", it buys. Each time it gets a "down", the strategy sells, usually at a small loss. If the market drifts sideways for some time, multiple "small" losses can add up to a significant loss. Since, by definition, the market is drifting sideways, a timing program will underperform the market while it takes these small losses. Some investors view the losses during sideways markets as "the cost of insurance" in order to be positioned for the large up moves and minimize the damage of major down moves.

Time spent in up, down and sideways markets

A study of the S&P 500 Index from January 1964 to February 1999 indicated that the market spent approximately 28% of the time in the "up" direction and only 7% of the time in the "down" direction. The remaining 64% of the time, the market moved in a sideways direction.

Study of market direction

Dates	1/64 to 2/99
Up direction	28.1%
Down direction	7.7%
Sideways direction	64.2%
Total	100%

This means that the periods when timing can add significant value occur only about 36% of the time. The rest of the time, timing will tend to be whipsawed. Despite these lopsided time period statistics, timing can add a lot of psychological comfort to the investor. To be a successful investor, one must sometimes do things that are uncomfortable. For instance, after seeing the market run up with reckless abandon, it's tempting to chase the buy and hold returns. Then, the investor gets into a buy and hold strategy and ends up suffering a sharp decline somewhere along the way that timing strategies might have helped avoid.

Another tough thing to do is to be patient. With the market in sideways activity for 64% of the time, it's tempting to get bored or irritated at the lack of substantial profits or even losses with a timing program. However, when the market moves up or down, the strategy should add some value. This means that roughly four out of 10 years, timing has added value. This also means that six out of 10 years, timing would struggle to add value. If a timing program is to be successful, over the long term the investor needs to have the patience to see the strategy through up, down and sideways periods.

10 Rules to Consider When Investing Your Money

WITH the scams in the industry, here are a few thoughts I would suggest the hedge funds and their investors consider:

1. **Never give your cash to the person managing it.** I always want to send a check to an independent administrator or custodian. The investment manager should have limited power of attorney on the account, not full power of attorney to deal with the cash. If the person managing it has access to the actual cash, they have the opportunity to steal or misappropriate it. With an independent custodian, there is no worry of that, unless the manager and the custodian get together to defraud the investors, which is why I have rule 2.

2. **Make sure the custodian and money manager are independent.** To help prevent collusion between the manager and the custodian, make sure they are reasonably independent. Sure they'll be friendly to each other, since they do business with each other, but you'd like the ownership structures of the two firms to be different. Ideally, only a small part of the custodian's business would be with that one manager, so you know the custodian has little incentive to fabricate statements or embezzle funds.

3. **Look for independent calculations of NAVs.** In many hedge funds, there's a tendency to let the manager value some of the instruments because "They're too complicated for an independent custodian to value," or "I can't let anyone calculate the NAV, since then they'd know our investment scheme." If that's the case, investors are letting the person managing the investments make up the track record. A number of legitimate, law-abiding managers, over the years, have had the opportunity to smooth their results by valuing their instruments in

a smoothed-out fashion, rather than having to deal with the gyrations of the actual marketplace and true mark-to-market prices. This makes Sharpe ratios higher than they really are and deludes both the manager and investor into thinking the investment is less risky than it really is.

4. **Make sure the fund has an annual accounting audit.** I would like it more if it's an independent firm that specializes in audits in the area of investing being considered. Some of the larger accounting firms may not have the specialized experience that certain smaller independent accounting firms may have. The important thing is that they work from independent statements from the custodian, not the manager, and verify the valuations of the instruments in the portfolio themselves, rather than relying on the manager to value the portfolio or provide the list of investments held. This is then a true check of the manager at least once per year. Auditors of the fund should be able to describe to the investor the process they used in auditing the fund.

5. **Monitor the investment in the environment in which it exists.** If you decide to buy a leveraged, long-only stock fund and it appears to be making big profits in a down stock market, be suspicious. If most of the market neutral managers are making between 10%–20% and yours is up 50%, be suspicious. Understand enough about the manager's strategy to know when and how profits will be made and when losses are to be expected. When something you don't expect happens, find out why. If something is not to your liking, move on at your first opportunity. There're thousands of other worthwhile deals out there.

6. **Understand how everyone in the deal is compensated.** Many investors simply look at the bottom line when making a purchase. Investors should read the legal paperwork on the investment fund and note who is involved in making money from the fund. I like to know each firm's role, how they perform their function and whether their fees reasonable for the contribution they'll be making to the fund. If somebody is making more than a typical fee from the fund, I get concerned.

7. **Ask yourself whether the returns you are considering are repeatable.** So many investors chase a great track record, never considering that maybe the environment the manager has just been through has matched up beautifully with his/her strategy. Maybe an environment that will do just the opposite is right around the corner. Understand enough about the strategy used to determine its consistency and repeatability before investing.

8. **There's risk with every investment.** If you haven't figured out the potential risk with an investment, you haven't looked hard enough. Every strategy has some risk, even if it's a low probability event. My experience is that higher probability, low severity risks are usually more manageable. It's those low probability, higher standard deviation moves that everyone ends up remembering for years due to phenomenal profits or extraordinary losses. Many investors and managers treat very low probability risk as "no risk", and that's dangerous because low probability, high severity events do happen.

9. **If these guidelines are not met, move on.** There are thousands of quality investment funds for investors to consider. If there is a fund you are considering that looks great, but doesn't meet all of the guidelines you desire to keep your funds safe, move on to another choice. Find a fund that does meet your safety guidelines. The investment you are considering may be completely legitimate and you may miss out on a great deal, but it also may be a disaster in the making. Why take on the stress, when there are so many legitimate funds that you can invest in that will meet your criteria?

10. **Legitimate funds should consider adopting these guidelines for themselves.** Serving as a NASD and NFA arbitrator, over the years I have found that the investing public has little ability to separate the legitimate deals from the scams. If the legitimate funds used independent custodians, pricing of their NAVs, independent accountants, and provided as much transparency as possible, then the scams would look suspicious by comparison. We'll never completely eliminate the scams, but we can make it more difficult for them to blend in with the legitimate managers.

Following all the above suggestions does not guarantee investing success. However, it should eliminate the majority of the nonsense we all too often see in the industry, such as fabricated statements, embezzlement, commingling of personal and investor assets, hiding losses, Ponzi schemes, etc. Successful investing is not easy. It takes a lot of work, discipline, resources and intelligence, and a little luck along the way can, of course, help the cause. These guidelines help make sure investors can worry about the return on their capital, not worry about the return of their capital.

The ETR Comfort Ratio

EVERY time I did research on new and better ways of trading for money management clients back in the day, or currently when I do it for myself, I look at statistics on return-to-risk to compare various approaches and ideas on trading strategies. With most research platforms you will end up with one or more of the following popular return-to-risk measurements:

- Sharpe ratio
- MAR ratio
- Return/max drawdown
- Return/average drawdown
- Treynor ratio
- Sortino ratio

All these ratios yield return-to-risk ratios where higher is better: more return for less risk.

Issues with measuring return-to-risk using these approaches

I need to start this discussion with some of the shortcomings of these popular return-to-risk definitions:

- **Sharpe ratio**: This uses return divided by standard deviations which presumes variations to the downside in the portfolio are equivalent to the upside. No client I have ever managed money for ever complained about the upside deviations in their account!

- **MAR ratio**: This ratio takes the annual compound growth rate over time and divides it by the maximum drawdown over that same history. The problem here is that the largest drawdown is taking into account only the depth of the SINGLE largest drawdown and doesn't look at all the other smaller drawdowns that may have been long in duration and cause clients to leave or traders to abandon a strategy due to fatigue or boredom.

- **Return/average drawdown**: This corrects the flaw mentioned in the MAR ratio on the single drawdown by using an average of all drawdowns. This might be more useful, but still doesn't consider the consistency of the returns and the impact the maximum drawdown could have on investors' psychology.

- **Treynor ratio**: This one is like the Sharpe ratio, but uses the beta of the portfolio relative to a suitable index, rather than standard deviation of the portfolio. If you pick various benchmarks, you will get a different beta versus the measured portfolio and therefore obtain a different Treynor ratio. I don't like the dependence on human judgment to select the suitable benchmark to create the beta of the portfolio.

- **Sortino ratio**: This is probably one of my favorites of the return-to-risk measurements often offered on the popular research platforms. This one starts with the Sharpe ratio, which uses the returns of the portfolio divided by the standard deviation (up and down) of the portfolio. It then changes the calculation to measure risk as only the downside deviations of the portfolio. This is closer to what investors and traders would view as risk, but doesn't consider time spent in the risk period.

A better way to calculate return-to-risk: the ETR Comfort Ratio

My 28 years of trading money for clients and almost 50 years managing my own portfolios taught me a lot about how an equity curve can cause the human trader to step into the investing process and modify, mess up, or cease using a trading strategy. It always amazes me to see those flashy track records out there with 50% drawdowns that show very excellent long-term Compound Average Growth Rate (CAGR) performances that are sold to investors. There is almost no way that any typical human being on the planet will stick around for that long-term record when they are seeing their portfolio down 50%. Most can't even last through more than a 15% to 20% down period!

So what causes clients and traders to pull the plug on a strategy due to performance? I would propose two different things: depth of a drawdown past what they are comfortable with and the time spent in those down periods. In other words, very few investors would be rattled with a 5% down period, but after a few years it would wear thin. On the other hand, a quick 30% down period might also cause many to abandon their plans immediately.

Having an engineering degree gives me some different views of what I see out there in the world, and the calculation of return-to-risk is one of them. To me, traders and their clients need comfort to keep doing what they are supposed to be doing. As soon as discomfort sets in past a pain or patience threshold, it is on to the next great idea.

I decided to use concepts from integral calculus to create a measure of the amount of discomfort caused by the magnitude of the down period AND the time spent in that period of discomfort. On the other side of things, I don't remember having any of my clients complain about making new equity highs. I started seeing the math develop into:

ETR Comfort Ratio = Amount of Comfort/Amount of Discomfort

Next, we need to include a few parameters that capture how much of a down return causes discomfort (Drawdown Return Threshold) and how long could a drawdown last before you or the money management client would have discomfort with the strategy (Drawdown Time Threshold). For most investors, maybe anything greater than 10% down or over six months in a drawdown would start making you think about changing what you are doing.

The Amount of Discomfort would be the sum of magnitude of the current drawdown during each period spent in that drawdown over the selected drawdown thresholds. As soon as the thresholds are exceeded, you would start summing each period's current drawdown value until the portfolio gets back to new highs, and you return to comfort levels.

The Amount of Comfort would be the reverse of the Amount of Discomfort. Whenever you get to new highs and move up from there, you would keep track of that surge up. The surge is the amount that the current upswing climbs above the current surge low after the last drawdown ended. You would sum every period's current surge until the next drawdown threshold is exceeded. At that point you would be back to summing the period's current drawdown to the Amount of Discomfort. The Amount of Comfort would essentially be the time and magnitude spent in periods of comfort.

The ETR Comfort Ratio would then be a simple ratio of the Amount of Comfort/Amount of Discomfort.

A simple example: T-Bills

If you think about the risk-free rate and ignore the dangers of runaway inflation or other risks, T-Bills are used in calculations all over the financial universe as the "risk-free rate." If the amount of time spent in a drawdown with a T-Bill with very short duration is near or at 0, then almost every day would be a comfort day, making a new high. Almost no days would be spent in down days, so the sum of those days would be near 0.

ETR Comfort Ratio (of T-Bills) =
A positive increasing number / 0 = infinity

In other words T-Bills should and do have a very high ETR Comfort Ratio.

Another example: S&P 500 Index

In a recently completed study, I pulled the S&P 500 Index monthly values going back to 1993, over 20 years at the time of writing this paper. I then created a simple spreadsheet to calculate the monthly ETR Comfort Ratio of the S&P 500 Index and a timed strategy of the S&P 500 Index over time. Two charts of the results can be seen opposite.

S&P 500 Index B&H vs. "Timed" using 50-day and 200-day moving averages

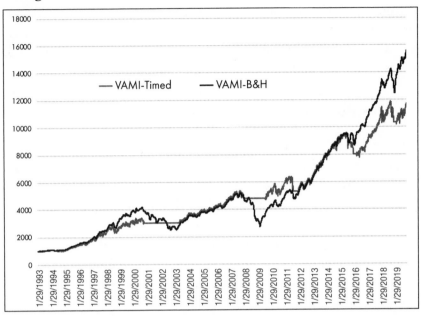

Timed vs. Buy and Hold Comfort Ratios

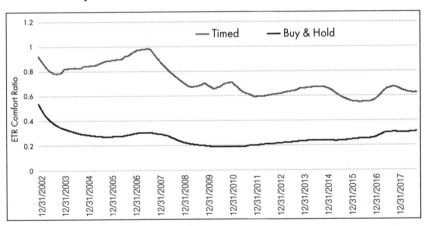

In the charts you can see that after you initialize the ETR Comfort Ratio back from 1993 through 2002, the index stays between 0.2 and 0.6 through the end of the data in 2019. The 2008 bear market really moved the index to extreme lows for the buy and hold approach. However, the timed approach suffered its worst low in 2017. From 2016 on, the comfort ratios of both the timed approach and the buy and hold have steadily moved higher with the bull market. The important thing to note is that the comfort ratio of the timed approach is far above the buy and hold over time. It's not surprising that investors feel more comfortable over the long run in a timed approach to investing rather the conventional "buy and pray" strategy that suffers occasional -50% drawdowns.

How do you calculate the ETR Comfort Ratio?

A small part of the very large spreadsheet used to create these charts is shown below. There are two conditions you are summing as you go. First, when in a drawdown that exceeds the Drawdown Return Threshold or the Drawdown Time Threshold, you keep summing the accumulated drawdown.

As soon as new highs are achieved, we start concentrating on the surge accumulation. The bottom of this surge is the previous equity high when the last drawdown started. When we get data for both the Accumulated Drawdown and the Accumulated Surge totals, we finally calculate our first ETR Comfort Ratio, realizing that it has limited data and that the index will stabilize with more up and down periods.

S&P 500 Index against the ETR Comfort Ratio

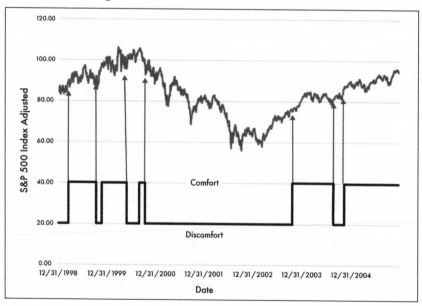

Date	Adjusted S&P 500 Index	Performance S&P 500 X Days	Daily Avg X Day Performance	VAMI of X Day Avg	VAMI Max Hi	Curr Draw Down %	Drawdown in Excess of Comfort %	Current Days in Drawdown	Comfort? Y or N?	Accum. Discomfort %	Surge Lows $	Current Surge %	Accum. Comfort %	Comfort Ratio
29/03/2019	279.82	1.81%	0.09%	13978.24	14239.66	-1.84%	0.00%	117	N	-45116%	13495.84	5.51%	13715%	0.304
01/04/2019	283.14	2.38%	0.11%	13994.07	14239.66	-1.72%	0.00%	118	N	-45117%	13495.84	5.51%	13715%	0.304
02/04/2019	283.28	2.80%	0.13%	14012.75	14239.66	-1.59%	0.00%	119	N	-45119%	13495.84	5.51%	13715%	0.304
03/04/2019	283.72	3.10%	0.15%	14033.46	14239.66	-1.45%	0.00%	120	N	-45120%	13495.84	5.51%	13715%	0.304
04/04/2019	284.48	4.01%	0.19%	14060.24	14239.66	-1.26%	0.00%	121	N	-45122%	13495.84	5.51%	13715%	0.304
05/04/2019	285.85	5.39%	0.26%	14096.35	14239.66	-1.01%	0.00%	122	N	-45123%	13495.84	5.51%	13715%	0.3039
08/04/2019	286.07	5.68%	0.27%	14134.51	14239.66	-0.74%	0.00%	123	N	-45123%	13495.84	5.51%	13715%	0.3039
09/04/2019	284.61	3.64%	0.17%	14159.01	14239.66	-0.57%	0.00%	124	N	-45124%	13495.84	5.51%	13715%	0.3039
10/04/2019	285.58	3.60%	0.17%	14183.3	14239.66	-0.40%	0.00%	125	N	-45124%	13495.84	5.51%	13715%	0.3039
11/04/2019	285.5	2.89%	0.14%	14202.84	14239.66	-0.26%	0.00%	126	N	-45125%	13495.84	5.51%	13715%	0.3039
12/04/2019	287.43	3.66%	0.17%	14227.57	14239.66	-0.08%	0.00%	127	N	-45125%	13495.84	5.51%	13715%	0.3039
15/04/2019	287.24	3.08%	0.15%	14248.42	14248.42	0.00%	0.00%	0	Y	-45125%	14239.66	0.06%	13715%	0.3039
16/04/2019	287.43	2.77%	0.13%	14267.24	14267.24	0.00%	0.00%	0	Y	-45125%	14239.66	0.19%	13715%	0.3039
17/04/2019	286.72	2.50%	0.12%	14284.2	14284.2	0.00%	0.00%	0	Y	-45125%	14239.66	0.31%	13715%	0.3039
18/04/2019	287.29	3.01%	0.14%	14304.66	14304.66	0.00%	0.00%	0	Y	-45125%	14239.66	0.46%	13716%	0.304
22/04/2019	287.54	1.95%	0.09%	14317.92	14317.92	0.00%	0.00%	0	Y	-45125%	14239.66	0.55%	13716%	0.304
23/04/2019	290.12	4.88%	0.23%	14351.19	14351.19	0.00%	0.00%	0	Y	-45125%	14239.66	0.78%	13717%	0.304
24/04/2019	289.48	4.73%	0.23%	14383.5	14383.5	0.00%	0.00%	0	Y	-45125%	14239.66	1.01%	13718%	0.304
25/04/2019	289.3	3.89%	0.19%	14410.13	14410.13	0.00%	0.00%	0	Y	-45125%	14239.66	1.20%	13719%	0.304
26/04/2019	290.65	4.92%	0.23%	14443.89	14443.89	0.00%	0.00%	0	Y	-45125%	14239.66	1.43%	13721%	0.3041
29/04/2019	291.1	4.69%	0.22%	14476.14	14476.14	0.00%	0.00%	0	Y	-45125%	14239.66	1.66%	13723%	0.3041

Date	Adjusted S&P 500 Index	Performance S&P 500 X Days	Daily Avg X Day Performance	VAMI of X Day Avg	VAMI Max Hi	Curr Draw Down %	Drawdown in Excess of Comfort %	Current Days in Drawdown	Comfort? Y or N?	Accum. Discomfort %	Surge Lows $	Current Surge%	Accum. Comfort %	Comfort Ratio
30/04/2019	291.25	4.09%	0.19%	14504.3	14504.3	0.00%	0.00%	0	Y	-45125%	14239.66	1.86%	13724%	0.3041
01/05/2019	289.06	2.09%	0.10%	14518.75	14518.75	0.00%	0.00%	0	Y	-45125%	14239.66	1.96%	13726%	0.3042
02/05/2019	288.44	1.82%	0.09%	14531.34	14531.34	0.00%	0.00%	0	Y	-45125%	14239.66	2.05%	13728%	0.3042
03/05/2019	291.26	2.66%	0.13%	14549.73	14549.73	0.00%	0.00%	0	Y	-45125%	14239.66	2.18%	13731%	0.3043
06/05/2019	290.06	1.96%	0.09%	14563.34	14563.34	0.00%	0.00%	0	Y	-45125%	14239.66	2.27%	13733%	0.3043
07/05/2019	285.22	-0.22%	-0.01%	14561.8	14563.34	-0.01%	0.00%	1	Y	-45125%	14239.66	2.27%	13735%	0.3044
08/05/2019	284.82	-0.44%	-0.02%	14558.77	14563.34	-0.03%	0.00%	2	Y	-45125%	14239.66	2.27%	13737%	0.3044
09/05/2019	283.96	-0.23%	-0.01%	14557.2	14563.34	-0.04%	0.00%	3	Y	-45125%	14239.66	2.27%	13740%	0.3045
10/05/2019	285.39	-0.07%	0.00%	14556.75	14563.34	-0.05%	0.00%	4	Y	-45125%	14239.66	2.27%	13742%	0.3045
13/05/2019	278.22	-2.55%	-0.12%	14539.07	14563.34	-0.17%	0.00%	5	Y	-45125%	14239.66	2.27%	13744%	0.3046
14/05/2019	280.73	-2.33%	-0.11%	14522.94	14563.34	-0.28%	0.00%	6	Y	-45125%	14239.66	2.27%	13746%	0.3046
15/05/2019	282.38	-1.69%	-0.08%	14511.23	14563.34	-0.36%	0.00%	7	Y	-45125%	14239.66	2.27%	13749%	0.3047
16/05/2019	284.99	-0.85%	-0.04%	14505.37	14563.34	-0.40%	0.00%	8	Y	-45125%	14239.66	2.27%	13751%	0.3047
17/05/2019	283.15	-1.25%	-0.06%	14496.76	14563.34	-0.46%	0.00%	9	Y	-45125%	14239.66	2.27%	13753%	0.3048
20/05/2019	281.28	-2.09%	-0.10%	14482.31	14563.34	-0.56%	0.00%	10	Y	-45125%	14239.66	2.27%	13756%	0.3048
21/05/2019	283.81	-1.30%	-0.06%	14473.38	14563.34	-0.62%	0.00%	11	Y	-45125%	14239.66	2.27%	13758%	0.3049

- Discomfort periods are accumulated in the column titled Accum. Discomfort.
- Comfort periods are accumulated in the column titled Accum. Comfort.
- Comfort ratio is the Accumulated Comfort/Accumulated Discomfort.

Spreadsheet example

In the spreadsheet example, you can see under the "Comfort Y or N?" column that I've shown a short slice of time starting with discomfort and switching to comfort. When in the discomfort period, the Accumulated Discomfort column increases each day by the amount of the current drawdown, while the Accumulated Comfort column stays constant. When in the comfort period, the Accumulated Comfort column increases each day and the Accumulated Discomfort column stays the same.

The Drawdown Return and Time Thresholds were set at -5% and 100 days for the example. Obviously, setting the Drawdown Return Threshold lower or increasing the number of days in the Drawdown Time Threshold would increase the ETR Comfort Ratio over this same period with this same instrument. This spreadsheet snippet is taken from an updated version of the ETR Trading Tools for Excel available on the enjoytheride. world website.

Conclusions and suggestions

I believe that the ETR Comfort Ratio truly measures more accurately what investors and traders are more concerned with when making decisions to "stay the course" or "pull the plug." The ratio by itself is probably not very useful. The number relative to other strategies or other management programs gives the user an ability to compare one against the other. The higher the ratio, the more comfortable the strategy. The lower the ratio, the more concern you would have investing in the strategy.

Remember that long-term track records are useless unless the client or trader continues the strategy and allows that track record to become a reality. One of my biggest challenges as a money manager was always trying to educate investors on good investment practices and convincing them to use those good practices over the long run, rather than making irrational, emotional decisions. One of the challenges that traders face is feeling comfortable with their strategy when it is being tested with adverse market conditions. Most investors and traders underestimate their tolerance for drawdown magnitudes and their patience with time elapsing without making any money.

The calculations can both be done over any period. The example I showed of the S&P 500 Index was daily data and covered over two decades. This is likely the easiest and most common way that the ETR Comfort Ratio should be used. I also know that many investors track their portfolio monthly from manager statements or brokerage statements, so I used 21 days for the calculation, which is roughly a month of trading days.

But since we live in the age of instant information, if everyone involved is going to be drilling down to daily data, then calculate the ETR Comfort Ratio daily if you wish. The math is the same and just as easy. However, my experience is that most investing clients are not able to look at daily data and not go crazy with the gyrations the market will put them through, and they would be better served to look at things once a month.

The ETR Comfort Ratio should be an excellent tool in developing investing/trading strategies, since it shows how comfortable it would be to use that strategy in investing/trading. Although the old disclaimer that historical simulation results certainly do not predict future profits is true, the historical volatility of a strategy tends to be a bit more consistent going forward and I would expect the Comfort Ratio of a strategy to be somewhat stable over time.

Investors have a propensity to invest when markets are strong and making new highs and panic after a drawdown, pulling their money off the table at market lows. Just like a lot of market measurements, the ETR Comfort Ratio may well lend itself to measuring investor/trader sentiment in that as the index gets to very high levels, the market is likely overbought, and investors are excited. And when comfort in the market is low, investors probably do not like the market, and it is likely in an oversold condition with the potential to move up from there. More research on using the ETR Comfort Ratio this way is warranted.

The Value Added of Asset Allocation Combined with Rebalancing

W HY deal with the hassle of an asset allocation strategy and rebalancing?

Every month we receive faxes, emails and calls from various clients adding, withdrawing and reallocating their investments with us. It's a lot of work for both our clients and ourselves. One of our programs is really a program-of-programs. Inside there are five distinct strategies, each with its own return-to-risk profile, margin requirement and personality. This challenges us with the same issue our clients have: How much to allocate to each investment and how often should we rebalance the allocations. Our goal at Trendstat is to improve return-to-risk ratios with these concepts, so I tested some of the aspects of managing the allocations in this study.

Background on the study

First, I needed a base case, so I took all five of the strategies we use and combined them together—20% each, with no rebalancing—and allowed them to individually produce profits and losses over the 86 months in which we had data.

I then structured three additional cases. First, I looked at staying with 20% in each strategy, but simply rebalancing it back to 20% each at the end of every month. This concept has been called a "Robin Hood" asset allocation approach, as it takes from the hot investment (the rich) and gives to the cold investment (the poor). I published a research paper on this concept back in June 1994 in MAR.

Next, I used our asset allocation strategy, based on the inverse of that investment's extreme volatility over any 20-day period in history. I've done studies internally that showed this to be more robust than traditional volatility-based allocation schemes. This is the way we currently allocate our flagship program-of-programs.

Finally, I combined rebalancing and the extreme volatility concepts together to determine the effect of having both in place. I used many standard measures of returns, risk and return-to-risk to analyze the cases amongst themselves.

Results of the study

I expected the base case to have a higher return and risk potential, since faster moving, successful strategies would grab a larger share of the portfolio in later years, due to not rebalancing the portfolio. This came through in the best month and the best and worst 12-month returns, with the base case receiving the best results of these statistics.

Rebalancing improved on the base case in every measure of return-to-risk and every measure of risk. This strategy also improved the percent of the months that were profitable over the period. Rebalancing the portfolio also produced the best annualized return over the period of any of the cases tested. It just makes good sense to keep the portfolio allocated the way you designed it to be allocated, even it is equally weighted, as in this case.

Using something better than equally weighting the portfolio is something all investors and fund of funds managers try to do. We have found some success using extreme volatility to set our allocations, since it robustly deals with those trying times where markets move with extreme volatility and large profits or losses can be had. This case presumed that we set the portfolio based on extreme volatility, then left it to float from there, with no rebalancing.

Table A: Various methods of allocation and rebalancing the portfolio

	Base Case	Rebalancing	Extreme Vol.	Both Concepts
Overall %	17.42%	**17.83%**	16.61%	17.25%
Max Drawdown	-11.73%	-9.91%	-8.57%	**-8.09%**
Best Month	**12.18%**	11.64%	11.36%	10.62
Worst Month	-9.08%	-8.87%	-7.87%	**-7.91%**
St. Dev. Mo.%	4.17%	4.00%	3.68%	**3.59%**
Return/Max. DD	1.48	1.8	1.94	**2.13**
Return/St. Dev	4.18	4.46	4.52	**4.8**
Best 12 Months	**41.21%**	40.12%	40.47%	38.55%
Worst 12 Months	**0.98%**	-1.31%	-2.87%	-3.47%
Sortino Ratio (0%)	1.88	2	2.01	**2.16**
Sharpe Ratio	1.26	1.31	1.26	**1.32**
% of the Mo. Profitable	65.10%	67.40%	67.40%	**68.60%**

Bold numbers highlight the best result across all cases.

Calculations used:

Sortino ratio = Annualized return/Annualized losing months only

Sharpe ratio = Annualized (monthly return – monthly T-Bill rate)/standard deviation of all rolling 12-month periods

This method also improved on every measure of return-to-risk except the Sharpe ratio and increased the percent of the months that were profitable over the base case.

Finally, I combined the asset allocation strategy and rebalanced it to the extreme volatility-based target allocations each month. This is the way we run our program-of-programs. With this case, we obtained the highest return-to-risk of any of the cases, the lowest risk measures of almost all of the cases and returns that were just slightly lower. The percent of the months showing a profit was the highest of all the cases.

What does this show us?

The first thing this study did was reaffirm my belief that a reasonable asset allocation strategy performs better than just throwing together an equally weighted portfolio. It also showed that rebalancing the portfolio consistently improves the return-to-risk ratios. The combination of the two is even more powerful and is clearly adding value to the overall portfolio.

Most investors and fund of funds managers have an allocation strategy, even if it's discretionary or arbitrary. However, in my experience as an investment manager, not all of our clients rebalance their portfolios as often as they could or should. This study helps provide investors with the motivation to use allocation and rebalancing techniques to help their clients' return-to-risk.

The second finding the study points to is the justification for individual investment managers to create more single manager, multi-strategy funds. The fund of funds, pool operators and family offices have known for years that diversifying their portfolios improved their return-to-risk ratios. However, one disadvantage that those investors have is that they have to allocate to commercially available strategies. That eliminates many strategies that are capacity limited, have minimums that are higher than the investor can afford or have such strange profit/loss profiles that the manager can't or doesn't offer it commercially.

The individual investment managers have no such limitation. They can use any number of strategies designed to diversify a single manager, multi-strategy program with little regard for what potential clients think about it. Their goal in the design stage of a multi-strategy fund is to combine together multiple strategies that they feel will deliver the best return-to-risk they can provide their clients. By developing sensible strategies, allocating to them with a reasonable plan and rebalancing them back to the targets frequently, the individual manager can definitely add value to the overall results, delivering the best return-to-risk possible from those strategies.

Thoughts on Good Investing Psychology in the Midst of Turmoil

REFLECTING on the few days from September 11 to September 17, 2001, I can't help thinking I've been watching some Bruce Willis movie. I just haven't seen the end of the movie yet, where the good guys take out the bad guys with severe prejudice. I usually look at life as a sort of movie where you can guess where the plot is going, but are sometimes surprised. You can remember where the plot has been, but it isn't going back there again. Just like in a movie, the only scene in life you can really see clearly is the one that is in front of you this instance.

Trading is a lot like that movie of life. The events on September 11 surprised and horrified. But, at that moment, and every other moment since then, good investors and traders have to focus on the moment at hand. Conditions may change, but focus on the current situation should never change. Predicting the future or reminiscing over the past may have its allure, and the media loves to speculate on the 50 different ways the world will evolve.

However, speculation on the future doesn't allow you to focus on what you should and can be doing right now. You cannot change trades you made last year, or do trades next week, because next week is not here yet. You can only make a trade or put in an order this moment. By focusing on the current scene of the movie of life, the trader can make sure he/she is properly positioned for the current volatile conditions.

Time Stocks Spent in Up, Down and Sideways Markets (2018 Update)

Purpose of the study

IN 1992 I did a study of how much time the market spends in up, down and sideways periods. It served several purposes at the time:

1. It put Trendstat's name in front of the money management industry.
2. It once again showed the value of timing the market in reducing risk.
3. It helped me personally be more patient when looking for returns from trading, since most of the profits come from very small percentages of the total time spent trading and from a small percentage of trades.

How the study was done

The original study analyzed data from January 1964 to July 1992. At the time, Trendstat's models were too complex to explain easily, so I used a simple exponential moving average (EMA) crossover model to create buy and sell signals. For this update to the study, I decided to create a fairly long-term, easy-to-execute strategy, using a 10-day EMA versus a 50-day EMA. When the 10-day EMA crossed the 50-day EMA to the upside, I rated that a "buy" signal. When the shorter EMA crossed the longer EMA to the downside, I considered it a "sell." I used only closing prices to keep it simple.

I then broke down all these signals into up, down and sideways markets. To do this, I assumed that an "up" market was any "buy" signal that created at least a +5% return. Any "sell" signal in which the market declined by at least 5% was considered a "down" market. If a signal gave somewhere between -5% to +5% return, the move basically went nowhere, so I rated the move a "sideways" market.

I then ran the program against the data, totaling the results by various measures.

Exponential moving averages

Let's digress a bit and define an exponential moving average (EMA). First you have to calculate a weighting factor based on the number of days you want in the moving average. The formula for the factor is:

Weighting Factor = 2 / (number of days=1)
For a 10-day EMA the Weighting Factor = 2 / (10+1) = 0.1818

The EMA each day is then calculated by taking today's close versus the average, times the Weighting Factor and adding it to the previous day's average. This adds only a fraction of today's data into the average.

Example: The average is 110 and today's close is 120. A 10-day EMA calculation would be:

New EMA = 110 + 0.1818 × (120 - 110) = 111.82

Results:

Trades	31	16	366	413	1	413
% of Trades	7.51	3.87	88.62	100	100	100
Number of days	5767	1862	12007	19636	19636	19636
% of days	29.37	9.48	61.15	100	100	100
Return %	464.03	206.56	-492.35	178.24		
CAGR %					6.90%	4.36%
Avg % Per Trade	14.97	12.91	-1.35			
Maximum					-56.78	-25.36

*Long only used in the timing calculation

Note: The database used for the study is 54.75 years' worth of data from 1/2/1964 to 10/1/2018

Conclusions

1. Most of the time (61%) was spent in sideways markets, where trend followers add little or negative value. However, the value lost on each trade was small (-1.35%.)
2. Value was added in both up markets (average +14.97%) and down markets (+12.91% losses missed).
3. Timing reduced risk (-25.36% maximum drawdown versus -56.78% for buy and hold).
4. Only 29% of the total time was spent in up markets.
5. Only 9% of the total time was spent in down markets.
6. The 10- and 50-day exponential crossover system measured about 6.5 round turns (13 trades) per year. That is about once per month, so the timing was not that active.
7. Buy and hold beat the timed approach due to a generally upward bias to stocks over the time period measured.
8. The long-only timing strategy produced a positive return, albeit lower than the buy and hold approach with a lot less risk in the process.

How I view the results:

The key to happy, long-term success in trading is to stay disciplined and stick with your strategy if it is performing the way you would expect it to. If you are in the stock market and 61% of the time you spend in markets that go nowhere, you have to realize you spend a lot of time trading going sideways. Timing only adds value in 39% of the time spent in the markets. Dial up the patience and give the strategy time to have enough up, down and sideways markets to see how it deals with each type of market. If it does as expected, then stay the course.

In addition, I find that many traders will abandon what they are doing when the going gets tough. I don't know many traders that will stick out a 56%+ drawdown, including me. So, from my experience as a money manager with clients and my experience as a trader, I can say that few I know stick around to actually experience a buy and hold strategy. There's just too much risk over time and sooner or later the strategy gets abandoned. Trading in order to position the portfolio with the trend makes more sense in keeping the trader mentally balanced, so that they can stick with the plan. They never put themselves into a position that goes against them for very long or for very much.

Timing the
Market Revisited

E'VE heard all the arguments.

The buy and hold believers will swear to you that you cannot beat the market by timing it. They'll point out the costs of timing. They'll point out all the money you could lose by missing out on the best days of the stock market, but conveniently avoid talking about missing the bad days and the effect on the investor's portfolio and psyche (more on that later). They'll make it sound complicated, too hard to do and something only an idiot would try.

We must be die-hard idiots then, because we've been timing the market in one form or the other for about 17 years now, and I would never feel comfortable buying and holding the stock market. Rather than saying timing doesn't work, financial advisors need to see it as just another way to approach investing with a different, lower risk return stream. I would argue that everyone should consider having some form of timed investment as part of their well-diversified portfolio.

Constructing a reasonable study of timing

The first step is to understand what constitutes a timing strategy. The following is a basic, yet effective timing strategy that anyone could do on a calculator or spreadsheet using a simple moving average, trend following strategy to time the market.

Moving averages allow us to focus on the overall direction of the market by minimizing the noise of daily market volatility. Think of a moving average of a combination of many days of prices. This reduces the effect any one day has on your decision-making. Many advisors use various moving averages, since these indicators ensure that investors participate in every major up move of the market.

Followed religiously, moving averages cannot miss out on a major move. Moving averages also get the manager out of down periods at some point, preserving part of the portfolio's value. The negative of using moving averages is that during sideways, volatile markets, moving averages tend to give a lot of signals that do not last long, leading to possibly frequent, brief trades, many at a loss. These trades are usually called whipsaws.

First, we create a slow, exponential moving average (EMA), using a 0.05 smoothing constant. The specific math formulae are at the end of the report. Next we use a fast average of 0.3 for a second EMA. As with most simple moving average strategies, when the faster moving average is above the slower one, we want to buy that investment. When it is lower than the slow average, we want to sell the investment. When out of the market, we credited the account with the yield on 3-month Treasury bills. and invested in the S&P 500 Index when in the market. Since the S&P 500 is an index, investors cannot invest directly in the index, however, a number of proxies exist for the S&P 500, including index funds and various exchange traded index funds.

One criticism of timing is that trading costs are not included in the studies, resulting in an overly optimistic return. An investor could buy and sell an S&P 500 Index fund for free, but I assumed a 0.2% per year cost for the expense ratio of an index fund, since I found a number of them available at that level of expense ratio. No-load funds have no other costs and can be purchased and sold easily using toll-free telephone calls or, in some cases, the internet.

Another criticism of many timing studies is that the money manager uses end-of-day prices to make the timing decisions, then credits the timed portfolio with the end-of-day price. Critics correctly point out that you wouldn't know you needed to buy until the end of the day, by which time it would be too late to buy. To correctly time the market, our simple example model will use the end-of-day data to calculate the buy and sell signals, then buy or sell at the close the next day. This would give us an entire day to call in the trade to the mutual funds.

I had data on the S&P 500 composite index, including dividends, going back to January 1960, and used that as my starting point for the study.

For a money market, I used the 3-month T-Bill yields from the Federal Reserve Economic Data (FRED) database over that same time period.

What is the potential objective of perfect timing?

The first thing we looked at was the potential benefit of timing the market. What if we had a perfect crystal ball each day? To get a feel for this, we took the S&P 500 Index and T-Bills. If the stock market went up by more than the T-Bill yield, we credited ourselves with the stock returns as measured by the S&P 500 Index minus the costs of the mutual fund. If T-Bills yielded more than the S&P 500, we credited ourselves with the interest on T-Bills.

Over the 41 years of the data we had, the annualized return for perfect timing was +142.7%. The Sharpe ratio, which measured the annual returns over a risk-free rate divided by the standard deviation of those returns, was 6.78—one of the highest ratios that I've ever seen. Of course, when timing the market in this ideal way, there was never a down day.

An investor owning one of those perfect crystal balls would have to make 4,648 trades over the 41 years, or about 113 trades per year—a lot of work. The best 250-day (about a year of trading days) rolling period for perfection would have been a smoking +372.3%, while the worst 250-day rolling period would still have been a lofty +50.3%.

Is this realistic? I would be the first in line to say definitely not, but it is helpful to give us a feel for the magnitude of the potential we are trying to achieve using any timing technique.

Performance of a simple timing strategy

To test the validity of timing, our simple strategy needed to be one an investor could quite easily execute, without a lot of strain or stress. The approach using two moving averages outlined above produced only 335 trades over the 41 years, averaging about nine trades per year. This would not be a heavy burden for most investors.

Not surprising to me, the simple timing strategy excelled through much of the '60s and '70s. By the late '80s, buy and hold had finally caught the timing performance. And during the bull market of the '90s, buy and hold was an easy winner.

Figure A shows a performance chart of a buy and hold strategy using the S&P 500 and T-Bills versus our simple timing approach. The '60s and '70s were a timing market and the timing strategy got off to a good start. The early '80s gave the investing public very high interest rates, so T-Bills did well during then. Finally, the buy and hold stock strategy did well in the late '80s and '90s, catching up to and exceeding the returns on the other two strategies.

Figure A: Performance of simple timing strategy vs. buy and hold (January 4, 1960–December 13, 2000)

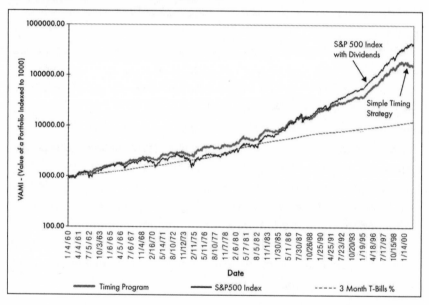

The simple timing strategy holds up well here against the buy and hold strategy. Interestingly, simple T-Bill growth was ahead of buy and hold as recently as 1983, some 23 years into the study. Yet, the timing strategy stayed ahead of our money market benchmark for most of the time period studied.

More results of the study

We looked at a number of different commonly used statistics on trades, return and risk to see how comfortable we'd be with the strategy. These results are found in Table A.

Table A

	Return/ year	Maximum drawdown	Longest time in drawdown in days	Average Hi to Lo drawdown	Trades	Trades/ year	Monthly st. dev.	Annual st. dev.
S&P 500 Index buy and hold	15.9%	-45.2%	1344	-5.6%	1	0	4.3%	19.1%
Three-month T-Bills	6.3%	0.0%	0	0.0%	166	4	0.2%	2.6%
Simple Timing Strategy	13.2%	-20.1%	777	-4.3%	335	8	3.3%	16.0%
Combined 50/50	14.7%	-30.8%	1089	-4.5%	336	8	3.6%	17.0%
Perfect timing	142.7%	0.0%	0	0.0%	4648	113	3.9%	19.3%

Data from January 4, 1960 through December 13, 2000

Not too many surprises here either. As I would expect, the risk of the timing strategy is lower than buy and hold due to being in T-Bills some of the time, which is considered risk-free. The timing strategy also keeps the maximum drawdown much more tolerable. In 1973–1974, the market fell by over 45%. Many investors bailed out with large losses and swore never to return to the stock market. Most investors of today either have never experienced this level of devastation to their portfolio, or simply have forgotten that the stock market can make these kinds of moves, or believe that the stock market has a different set of rules now.

The simple timing strategy cut the maximum length of time an investor would have to suffer through a drawdown to 777 days (about 2.1 years) from 1,344 days (about 3.7 years) with a buy and hold S&P 500 strategy. Average drawdowns were much lower with timing as well, giving the investor a more comfortable ride through the rough periods for the stock market.

Table B

	Return to maximum drawdown	Sortino ratio	Sharpe ratio	Correlation to S&P 500
S&P 500 Index buy and hold	0.35	3.46	0.49	1.00
Three-month T-Bills			0.00	-0.04
Simple timing strategy	0.65	3.37	0.42	0.73
Combined 50/50	0.48	3.54	0.48	0.73
Perfect timing			6.78	0.81

Data from January 4, 1960 through December 13, 2000

Shown in Table B are some return-to-risk measures. The timing strategy is the winner with the return-to-maximum drawdown ratio. What this shows us is that the timing strategy was able to produce more return for a unit of maximum drawdown suffered by investors. The Sortino ratio, which ratios return over the losses from just the losing months, was close, with a slight edge to the buy and hold strategy. Although possibly the most popular, my least favorite return-to-risk is the Sharpe ratio. It implies a normal distribution of returns, something which actively managed strategies almost never have. Buy and hold has a better Sharpe ratio than the simple timing strategy.

The best Sortino ratio of all is created by combining 50% buy and hold with 50% timing strategy. This provides enough of a different return stream that the Sortino ratio of the entire portfolio is improved slightly over the timing strategy. The simple timing strategy had a 0.73 correlation to the S&P 500. Even those critics of timing should realize the beneficial effect to an overall portfolio in introducing a different, less correlated return stream into any mix of investments.

They were the best of days, the worst of days ...

I think I've seen the same study quoted 15 times criticizing timing strategies for what they potentially give up by missing the best 10 or 20 days of the stock market's movements. Interesting perhaps, but what's wrong with flipping that on its head and looking at the possibility or benefit of missing the worst days the market has dealt us over time?

In Table C, we see that the worst day the market experienced in our database was the October 19, 1987 crash for a loss of −20.4%. Many investors may not recall sitting in front a quote machine, like I did, watching the Dow go down 5 points every few seconds and realizing that what you were looking at was about one hour behind reality due to the volume of panic selling. The banks had to intervene the next day to provide liquidity and help prevent a breakdown of the financial system as we know it. Many thought the whole system was crumbling. Now sharp down moves are thought to be buying opportunities. Sell-offs are "profit-taking." Does anyone really believe that everyone is taking profits when the market declines?

Table C

	10 best days total %	10 worst days total %	Single best day %	Single worst day %	Best rolling 250 days %	Worst rolling 250 days %
S&P 500 Index buy and hold	53.7	−77.3	9.1	−20.4	74.0	−41.6
Three-month T-Bills	1.6	0.1	0.2	0.0	15.6	2.8
Simple timing strategy	37.9	−49.5	5.2	−6.8	64.4	−17.1
Combined 50/50	39.3	−56.5	5.2	−10.2	67.6	−28.3
Perfect timing	53.7	0.1	9.1	0.0	372.3	50.3

Data from January 4, 1960 through December 13, 2000

Our simple timing strategy noted the down direction of the market leading up to the crash and was safely tucked away in T-Bills 10 days before the day of the crash. The worst single day suffered by the timing strategy was −6.8%, about what investors are now used to seeing their tech stocks move each day.

What the timing critics don't realize, or don't want to talk about, is the devastating effect of losses on a portfolio. The 10 worst days of the buy and hold strategy during this period cost investors a total −77.3%, while the timing strategy's 10 worst days total was only −49.5%. Looking at the impact of both the 10 best and 10 worst days, the buy and hold portfolio yields −23.6%. Had the simple timing strategy missed participating in the 10 worst and the 10 best days, the result is a +12.0% advantage to timing.

There clearly is more emotional impact when markets drop than when they increase, probably due to the panic in down markets being scarier to investors than their enthusiasm when markets go up.

If we look at 250-day rolling periods, the advantage stays with timing. Adding the total of the best 250-day periods to the worst 250-day periods, timing turned in a 47.3% total gain, while the buy and hold came in +32.4%. Looking at all the periods that make headlines, both to the upside and downside, I have to conclude that a timing strategy is a more sensible approach because it offers less risk, less emotional stress and comparable returns.

Annual returns

I like to study the down periods, because it is those periods that stress out investors and cause them to abandon their investment plans. Ignoring investor behavior is a major oversight in many academic studies. The reality is that investors don't like losses and make emotional decisions, especially when seeing losses in their portfolio. To analyze down periods, we plotted the annual returns of each 12-month period (from February to the end of January) in Figure B. The buy and hold strategy had eight losing 12-month periods, while the simple timing strategy totaled seven losing periods. More important, you can see visually that the magnitude (and therefore the pain and stress) of the timing strategy was far less than some of the larger downs of the buy and hold strategy.

Figure B: Annual returns of simple timing strategy against buy and hold and T-bills (January 4, 1960–December 13, 2000)

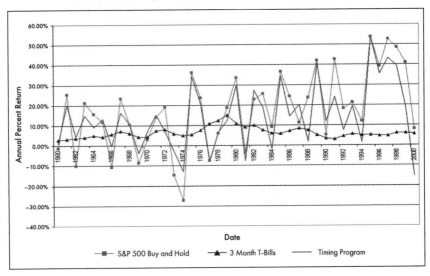

Sorting the monthly returns

Another way to profile two different strategies is to sort their returns from worst to best and compare the profiles. In Figure C, we plotted the sorted monthly returns from both strategies. You can see that the timing strategy cut out some of the risk of the really bad months and gave up a little performance in the upside months. On a monthly basis, both strategies have about the same number of positive and losing periods.

Figure C: Sorted S&P 500 buy and hold vs. simple timing strategy (January 4, 1960–December 13, 2000)

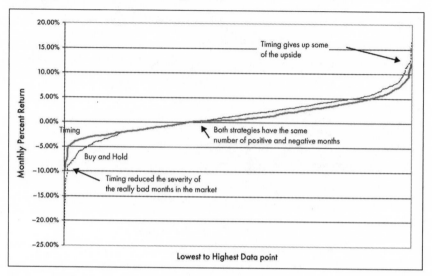

The real reason that timing helps the investor
=

I believe that the most important reason to consider timing for a portion of your clients' portfolios is one that I cannot develop using these statistics. Twenty-four years of managing client assets has shown me that investors like to chase hot returns, buying into something that has done well recently and selling that investment out at lower prices after a bad period of performance. This is why numerous studies have shown that actual investor timing of assets has hurt their overall performance.

Why then would we want to time the market, if all the studies have shown that actual client timing is so poor? The answer is that actual client timing has been driven more by investor psychology than by logic. Our simple timing strategy (or more sophisticated ones used by many investment managers) forces the investor to buy when the market is moving up, not question the direction or how long the move will last. It forces the investor to sell out of the market after he's made large profits, is euphoric with the market, but the market starts to move lower. It helps to provide the discipline that the typical investor lacks.

Another psychological aspect that drives me to use timing techniques on my portfolio is understanding myself well enough to know that I could never sit in a buy and hold strategy for two years during 1973 and 1974, watch my portfolio go down −48% and do nothing, hoping it would come back someday. Timing strategies give me the psychological lift that allows me to react to market risks and modify my exposure to those risks over time. It's empowering to be able to know that I can cut losses short and let gains run. It keeps my investing mind concentrated on doing the right thing each day, rather than succumbing to all emotional swings that most investors go through in up and down markets.

If an investor's mental process is not sharp and disciplined, the market has ways of teaching that investor what risk really is. Unless investors subscribe to the paradigm that the "new" economy has created a stock market that is a money machine and always goes up, then they should consider professionally managed timing strategies for at least a portion of their diversified portfolio.

Math used in creating an exponential moving average (EMA)

Today's Fast Moving EMA = Yesterday's Fast Moving EMA + 0.3 X (Today's price − Yesterday's Fast Moving EMA)

Today's Slow Moving EMA = Yesterday's Slow Moving EMA + 0.05 X (Today's price − Yesterday's Slow Moving EMA

Risk Control System

Excerpted from, "Guide to Becoming a CTA," by Dean E. Lundell

New position risk

1. Determine trade entry price via trading system.
2. Determine stop-loss price.
3. Convert the price difference between the entry point and the stop-loss point into dollars per contract. {Example: Buy gold at $400 per oz., with stop at $390 (trailing with a 10-day moving average of closing prices). Account size: $200,000.} (400 - 390) x $100/point = $1,000 risk per contract
4. Determine risk per trade as a percent of equity. $200,000 x 1% = $2,000 per trade
5. Divide risk per trade by risk per contract to determine number of contracts to buy for the position. $2,000 risk per trade: $1,000 risk per contract = 2 contracts

Ongoing risk exposure

1. Determine risk limit per existing trade as a percent of equity, e.g., 2.5%.
2. Determine risk per contract based on changes in price and stop-loss point. (450 - 405) x $100/point = $4,500
3. Determine allowable risk based on portfolio equity. ($210,000 x 2.5% = $5,250)
4. Determine number of contracts to hold by dividing allowable risk by risk per contract. $5,250 ÷ $4,500 = 1.167 (rounded down to 1)

To make this relatively simple risk management system a bit more complicated, you could get into fancy allocations among a variety of markets or into controlling total portfolio risks. Personally, I think that is like squeezing the last drop out of the sponge.

Measuring Futures Volatility

Excerpted from "Guide to Becoming a CTA," by Dean E. Lundell

Daily volatility

1. Take the open, high, low and closing prices of the last two trading days.
2. Determine the market's "true range" of price movement over the last 24-hour trading period by measuring the difference between the higher of yesterday's close or today's high vs. the lower of yesterday's close or today's low.
3. Convert "true range" in tick to dollars per contract to determine average daily volatility. $3 average true range X $100 per point = $300 average volatility per contract
4. Average these figures over several days, perhaps 10 or 20, depending on your trading strategy.
5. Calculate contracts by first multiplying account equity by the percent you wish to limit volatility to (say 1%). Then divide this number by the volatility per contract above to determine the contracts to hold. ($2000,000 x 1%) / $300 = 6.67 contracts (rounded down to 6)
6. Compare this answer to the number of contracts as determined by the ongoing risk exposure and take the smaller of the two.

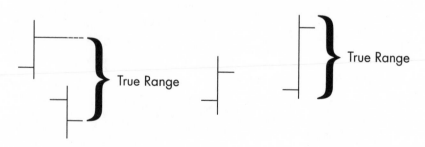

The Logic of Trend Following and How to Improve Your Trader Psychology with Market Wizard Tom Basso

INTERVIEW WITH TOM BASSO
BY AARON FIFIELD, JULY 22, 2015

Aaron: I reread your *New Market Wizards* interview and I listened to a bunch of your interviews on Michael Covel's podcast. They're all really insightful and so I'm excited to hear what you're about to share with us today.

Would you give a quick snapshot of who you are and what you're most well known for?

Tom: Sure. I'm of course the former creator and President of Trendstat Capital Management, which had about a 28-year run or so. I started out as a chemical engineer and got into trading, and one thing led to another. First I was trading stocks, and I got into bonds a little bit and traded a few options. I got into futures trading, expanded that to about 80 different markets in futures and eventually got into currency trading, which is the bulk of my money at the end, but we still traded mutual funds and futures.

At our peak we handled about $600 million of other people's money. So we were registered as trading advisors and registered investment advisors in the US.

Shut that down in 2003, enjoying retirement the last 12 years or so.

Aaron: That's a really impressive way to kick this off. I'm keen to hear how you very first got into trading and what initially attracted you to the financial markets.

Tom: As a chemical engineer by background, I realized that there was boom and bust in the United States economy. Every time there was a boom they'd hire engineers; and every time there was a bust they'd lay them off. Not wanting to get laid off and at least wanting to have a backup plan, I decided I had better save some money as I was earning it.

As that got to be a little bit of a larger quantity of money, I decided I should do something with it rather than simply sticking it into the bank. Some friends of mine that were also chemical engineers would talk about the stock markets at lunch, so that intrigued me and we started a stock portfolio so I could participate in the conversations as well.

That led to the investment club, where we ended up eventually running the club, and that ended up in a small investment advisory business. I teamed up with another couple of fellows and got that going. That grew into a substantial size, and I eventually sold my share of that company and formed Trendstat. Trendstat was my way of trying to not only manage my own money, but manage my client monies as well.

We just kept growing that over time and evolving in complexity, number of markets and so on until we became the success that we became.

Aaron: You mention that you started out as a chemical engineer. Were there any skill sets that you learned as an engineer which you applied to trading?

Tom: The most obvious one was something called process engineering. That is one of the first lessons you learn as a chemical engineer. The old pipeline comes into the tank, the tank is full of water, and there's a pipeline going out of the tank.

You learn how different flows coming into the tank will fill the tank over certain amounts of time, and you learn that flows going out take the water out over time. When you have them coming in and going out at different rates then you need to be able to calculate how much water is going to go up or down in the tank.

So process engineering in my mind always becomes stuff coming in, stuff being processed, and stuff shipping out. Trendstat Capital

Management was a perfect example of that. We had all sorts of downlinks and internet connections bringing in data continuously. In some cases tick by tick.

Then we were an operation that did nothing but process that information. So we had 40 computers and 10 people at our max that were just doing nothing but crunching a lot of data. Then there's the flow out. The orders, the communiqués, the updates to websites and all that. To me that's just process engineering: Bring in the information, process the information, ship information out.

The faster, the better and more efficient you can do that, the better off you're going to be.

Aaron: Sticking with that journey as you were starting out, if we were to zoom in on your first few years, what do you recall your experience being like?

Tom: The first thing that comes to mind brings a smile, because the first few years I would say were pretty much losses and me making mistakes and just sort of wandering and trying to find my way. I learned lots of things like fundamentals, and I took several newsletters, and I read opinion after opinion to the point where I was totally confused.

I realized that sooner or later a trader has to take individual responsibility for what he or she is going to do. The only way you're going to do that is to simplify everything down so that you can say, "This is how I'm going to trade. I'm going to take this data, I'm going to examine it or process it, and there's going to be a flow of orders that goes away from me." When I do that efficiently and religiously, with discipline, that's where I'm going to be able to analyze whether that approach is working or not working, modify it if it's not working, improve it and keep getting better and better as a trader.

The first couple of years were actually losing years. It required a tremendous amount of foresight, strategic knowledge, and patience on my part to just keep doing it, because how many times do you want to beat your head against the wall before you stop? There was certainly plenty of that in my first few years.

Aaron: Most of us will probably never forget our very first trade—do you remember your first trade and how did that turn out for you?

Tom: I don't remember the specific trade, but I remember that it was a stock that I bought, and I think I bought it based on somebody having a hot tip. I want to say it was aluminum. I realized well into the trade that I have no idea how this particular tip that I was given had anything to do with the financial well-being of aluminum and that I had no idea how to get out of the thing once I got into it. I didn't even have the ability to chart it or do anything, so I just really felt like completely a fish out of water. I had no idea what I was doing. I realized it fairly quickly and thankfully did not lose too much money on that one. I did lose a little, but I thought it was an interesting educational experience.

Aaron: Is it true that when you very first started you actually lost money for five years consecutively?

Tom: That would be my commodities trading. I think it was the fourth year where I at least broke even. The first year I lost money, the next year I lost less money, the next year lost less money, and then finally broke even. It probably took me about four or five years, roughly, to where I was actually producing a reasonable profit.

Aaron: How were you able to lose money for four or five years yet continue trading? What was it that motivated you to not give up?

Tom: How was I able to keep doing it? I was a chemical engineer. I actually had a day job, I was making good money; we were in great demand back in the oil embargo days in the '70s and '80s. I ended up with a nice job, lots of promotions. I was highly ranked in my daytime job. I always got the best raise, the best promotion, and eventually I moved over into the business side of the chemical industry and was still trying to advance down that road while I was trying to become a better trader at the same time.

Because of that, I had cash flow. And because I always kept my trading very small and as I was trading and losing small amounts of money, I was easily able to not only replace the losses, but to increase the size of my account—to improve diversification, to improve the numbers of volatility and risk controls, and things that I was learning how to do at the early stages. Some of that just requires more capital, and I just worked real hard and tried to save as much as I could and keep adding to the account.

I was able to keep going because when I looked back at the end of each year, I could always see that I had made progress. I had made less mistakes, I lost less money, I had captured more of the types of moves that I was trying to capture.

It kept me thinking that I'm on the right path and I just need to keep refining it and getting better and getting more diversified and keep my costs down; and little by little I finally got there. It took a long time.

Aaron: Is there any way that you feel as though you could have potentially shortened that learning curve from the point of first starting out to where you reached a level of profitability?

Tom: In today's world, the brokers will give you free practice trading software that would allow you to run tests for very little or no money as an inducement to get you to trade your account through them. Interactive Brokers comes to mind, interactivebrokers.com, but there're others too.

There's lots of software that you can either buy or use in various levels of sophistication that will allow you to test certain ideas out and cover a variety of data. In my day, I literally had *The Wall Street Journal*. I saved every one religiously. When I did a study, it would be pulling out *The Wall Street Journal* day after day after day and sticking it on a piece of paper because mini computers, micro computers, hadn't even been invented yet.

So I'm doing this all by hand. I'm using chart paper and I'm running a study over a course of a couple of years of data. It would take me an entire weekend to just try to run some idea on one particular market for maybe a few years of data. It was cumbersome, and tediously slow to get it done. But I knew that once I had certain things done, I could use that and understand what I was going to get on the good side and what I was going to get on the bad side.

It also forced me as a trader to live in the moment of those trades, day by day in the historical data. Today, traders have such fancy, sophisticated software that you could run 20 years of data against 60 different markets, and you'd get some number at the end that says you made 12%. There's no understanding of how that 12% was made in the detail. It's just the final page of the study that comes out and gives you all these fancy statistics and you say, "Oh, I like that; I'll do that."

But you don't live with the trades day by day and realize the types of things that could have happened intra-trade that you have to be able to psychologically live with. Well, because I was doing everything by hand, I ended up being able to really understand how a trade evolved day by day.

Aaron: Was there anything else you were doing to educate yourself on the subject of trading?

Tom: I read a lot of books. We also had a lunchtime crowd that would exchange ideas. Those were the two ways I kept expanding my brain.

Aaron: During this period up to, say, your first 10 years in the markets, were there any points that forever changed the way you approached trading? Any aha moments, realizations or hard lessons that will forever stick with you?

Tom: There was one that I talked to Jack Schwager about in *The New Market Wizards* that is etched on my memory and involved the Hunts' corner on silver way back when. I can't even remember the year anymore; I must say it was in the '80s. I was long in silver as I was supposed to be and at that time my futures account might have been between $70,000 and $100,000. It had gotten to be a decent-sized account, but it was relatively small and all of a sudden silver starts screaming upward.

I forget how many contracts I got, maybe four or five. Looking at my equity in my account—today it's $125,000, then it's $150,000, then $175,000, then $200,000. It got all the way up to $500,000 on just one trade. And my account was going up and down, $25,000 to $50,000 a day as it got to the top and got frothy. Darn it, I'm a good trend follower at that point. I'm going to stay with this trade, and let the trade run, let the winner run. Cut the losses short. That's the rules, you've got to do it, and I was just so disciplined about it.

By the time it got back to its stop loss point, which I had moved up and followed the trend, I ended up netting out about a $250,000 account. On the surface, what's wrong with that? Right, we started with $50,000 or $75,000 and we ended up with $250,000. That's a good trade. It certainly was very profitable.

But when I sat back at the end of it, and I thought of the nerves that I had to put up with, to live through that trade, I thought, "Wait a second. Should I have really had five contracts or whatever it was throughout this entire trade? Or would it have made more sense, when the markets got insane, to hold less of that position? So that as a portfolio, all of my instruments would have a somewhat equivalent ability to produce profit or to create loss, and they would be able to diversify each other a little bit.

In this one case, the silver so dominated my portfolio that I might as well not even have been trading anything else. That didn't seem right to me, so I started doing a lot of research on volatility as a percent of equity in my portfolio, From that point on, I started creating the early stages of what Trendstat eventually very successfully used over the years, which was our volatility controls. Along with that, the risk controls evolved, and we used those at Trendstat as well. This was limiting the risk of the particular market to my portfolio and limiting the volatility that it contributes to the portfolio—both as a percent of equity.

Once I had those two things in place, performance got a little more predictable and consistent, and profitability got a little better. I guess it allowed me to put the proper number of contracts on so that one market didn't dominate the losses too much. I ended up ultimately with margin as a percent of equity controls in a couple of instances in Trendstat. We had the ability then to put together real portfolios that had real diversification, that had real abilities to have all the markets self-contribute to the profits or the losses.

That was a real aha moment to me, because living through that silver trade sure was a way to keep yourself up at night.

Aaron: Can you elaborate on what you really mean by volatility control as a percentage of equity? How could other traders adapt this to better manage their capital?

Tom: It's easy to do. I'll give you the exact formula. Take a market and figure out for one futures contract how much the highest high of the day and the lowest low of the day is worth in range in dollars, or whatever currency you're living with. In our case, US dollars.

The number you come up with is the volatility of one contract for that market for that day. I use a 20-day exponential average of that daily volatility, but you can use whatever you want; it all works similarly. So that gives me how much this thing is moving up and down in the last 20 days. Is it moving up and down for a contract $1,000? Is it moving up and down $200? Is it moving up $500? Whatever it is, it's just telling you that this is how much this thing is moving. It is going to contribute that much per day when it's going your direction, and it's going to potentially hurt you that much a day if you're in the wrong way.

Once I have that number then I just divide it by the dollars of equity in my account. Let's say I'm trading $100,000 and that particular market was moving highest high to lowest low at $1,000 in any one day. That one contract would then have a 1% volatility to equity: $1,000 divided by $100,000.

At Trendstat, for some 80 different markets we ultimately traded, each market would have a very specific level of volatility that it would be capped at. We would never let it get above that. Every day the computers would take in the data, re-crunch the 20-day moving average of the volatility, re-crunch the equity that we now have because we've either made money or lost money today, so the equity's changed.

You then come up with a new percent equity for percent of volatility to equity and in every single one of the 80 markets it would compare them to the allowed limit of each of those markets, and it would give us a set of orders to peel off markets if we ever had any that got over the volatility level. We would just sell them off at market the next day.

Aaron: During those early years did you always envision yourself as reaching the high levels of success that you were able to achieve? I'm interested to know if you had that long-term vision that you were working toward. You knew where you wanted to get; it was just a matter of how you were going to get there?

Tom: I didn't even picture that I would be a professional money manager when I started out. I was a chemical engineer. I was simply looking for a way of trying to manage some money on the side, and I assumed that if I was successful at running my own portfolio, I perhaps could retire a few years early from being a chemical engineer.

I was happy in the early stages of being a chemical engineer. I was paid very well for it. Chemical engineers, when they came out my year in '74, were one of the highest-paid engineering disciplines because of the oil embargoes and everything.

Life was pretty good for a young, single 20-something that's making more money than he's spending, and it's piling up in his account, and he is learning how to trade. I just assumed it would be a side portfolio in that I would somehow be able to increase my net worth and I'd have the backup in case I was ever laid off.

Little by little, as people found out I was having some success with my own portfolio, the investment club said, "Hey, why don't you do what you're doing for yourself with some of our money?" That led to a certain limit on the number of people I could do that for before all of a sudden I'd gotten registered as an investment advisor and was then running into two other friends that ended up getting into the investment advisory business with me.

I still figured we'd just do this on the side and do it part-time at night or on weekends, and it'd be a second source of potential income. But it was still just a way to manage the money and defray the expenses of taking all these services, the costs to registration in the US. There's some money involved in that.

What ended up happening, much to my amazement, is on a part-time basis we ended up making enough money off of our business so that we could pay one salary full-time.

So I said to my two partners, "You guys have kids and all that, and you can't really travel, you're tied down a bit more. I don't have any children, I've got a lot of flexibility. How about if the company pays me the salary that I'm making now at the chemical company and allows me to leave and open up the offices, and let's take this seriously and make it a full-time successful business?"

They agreed. I left, started everything, started traveling and meeting clients, and putting business on the books, and creating computer systems and hiring secretaries and signing office leases and doing all the things that you have to do. One thing led to another, and pretty soon I've got the second partner out, and before long the third partner joins us. We had more staff. The whole thing becomes a wild success.

Aaron: Talk to us about how you were trading at Trendstat. I believe that it was a totally systematic operation, so can you shed some light on that topic?

Tom: The name of the company was coined by myself, just trend following statistics abbreviated to Trendstat: s-t-a-t is statistics, and trend is the trend following or trend of the markets.

I felt like if you could collect lots of data on lots of different markets, determine the trends and then always position the portfolios in line with whatever that trend was, then over time there were going to be large movements, large trends that ended up paying your way for the most part.

A good statistic I would cite was in the first year at Trendstat, I did an analysis of where we made money and where we lost money, and I actually rated the trades from the most profitable trade during the year all the way down to the largest loser of the year. We were running about 30-something percent reliable in terms of our trading—that is to say 30% of our trades would be profitable, and 70% of them would be losers.

But it turns out that one year, two trades were so largely profitable that if you had not gotten those two trades in your portfolio you would have broken even for the year. That's how lopsided it was to the two trades that ended up being so blockbuster and so unbelievable. You had to have them in your portfolio; if you didn't you were just going to break even that year.

That got me thinking—I've got to make sure, with no excuses, that I always get every one of those two or three large trades every year. Those are going to pay the way, and the rest of it is a whole bunch of hard work to get nowhere.

That was really what led me to kind of just expanding the number of markets that I traded. If you welcomed more markets, there were that many more opportunities to catch those one or two trades in those particular markets. I never knew which market ahead of time or which trade I was making was going to be that big winner, but I wanted to make sure that I had as many chances of catching them as possible.

So I just kept buying more and more computers. At the peak, including myself as an engineer, we had three full-time computer experts that were doing everything from programming to hardware, to keeping the networks running and backing things up to backup facilities off-site. All sorts of things.

It became a data processing facility really. A lot of people used to think of me—and still do—as a trader. A lot of times when I was in the middle of Trendstat, I was thinking of myself as the president of this data processing company while I was a trader. I realize, looking back at it, I definitely was a trader. I had to create all these programs, I had to tell my programming people what I was trying to go for, and that was being a trader. But if you'd walk up and follow me around all day, you'd kind of be wondering how would anybody think that I was a trader.

Aaron: That's really interesting how you called yourself or the company just a data processing hub, instead of what you typically think of when you think of a trader. That's quite funny.

Generally speaking, was there any human interaction with the trading systems during a typical trading day at Trendstat?

Tom: No, there was zero. We built lots and lots of computer programs that would take data in. We would run the programs once a day against that data and then decisions would be made by the algorithms that we had built into the computers. Prints would come off and the human beings would just scan them to look for any kind of computer malfunctions or data malfunctions or anything that looked strange to anybody.

That would be the last chance we would have to catch an error—perhaps created by poor programming. But once we knew that everything looked normal, the data looked normal, the data passed all the data checks that we did, the orders were created, hit the button, and out they go.

All of that was automated. The only thing the human beings would have to do was start the process to run the orders, visually scan them to see if anything looked strange, and hit a button to transmit them. That was the only thing the humans did.

Aaron: Trendstat was in full effect in the '90s, correct?

Tom: Yes, in various stages.

Aaron: During that time period, was this systematic, automated approach common amongst money management firms, or was this quite new to the space of money management? Was the technology that you were using reasonably cutting edge for the time?

Tom: I would say that "cutting edge" means very different things to different people. If it was at all cutting edge, it would be something like us trying to take a longer-term trading strategy across a lot of markets in order to automate that process. I do believe that during the '90s there were automated traders out there, but they were probably more intra-day trading and straddle trading, pairs trading, those types of things. It seemed like a lot of the automation was concentrating more on the very short term and we were just the opposite, concentrating on the fairly long term, but doing it in a systematic way. We were probably unusual in that regard.

Aaron: What was the initial appeal that attracted you to a systematic approach?

Tom: I would call it laziness—human being laziness. When I was doing my initial work and I had to have my chart paper out, burn my eyes up every night trying to go through what the markets did and put in my new data and figure out where my orders were and create some kind of a fact fax, and then ship that to the trading desk and have them put my orders in for the next day—it was a lot of work.

When personal computers came out and I was an engineer with my background and I knew how to program, I thought, "Well, why don't I get me one of these things, and I'm just going to program the ability to put the data in and pull it down from some place and program the computer to do what I do every day. Then it'll generate a set of orders and then maybe I could print them out and put them in a fax machine."

I later on figured out that there's these things called fax cards and that I can take the print and take it right to the fax machine and out to the order desk. Little by little, I kept eliminating my jobs. I developed this philosophy that there's two forms of human endeavor, so to speak.

There's the artistic, creative side, which I think everybody loves to do—the artsy side, the inventive side. Then there're a lot of things we do as human beings that are just stuff a machine can do and is very repetitive and doesn't require any unbelievable brain behind it—if you can put down in a rule-based way exactly how you're doing what you're doing, then you can have a machine do the same roles. You just have to program it into the machine.

What I tried to do at Trendstat is keep everybody as much as possible working on the creative and inventing side of things and let our computers save us the drudgery of every day. That was the philosophy.

Aaron: You've talked about your systematic approach, but I believe your actual trading method was very much based on trend following. What was it about the trend following approach that you adapted that meshed with your personality so well? What are some of the key benefits to this approach that you saw?

Tom: One of them was that a lot of the major mutual funds and brokerage firms constantly kept saying, "It can't possibly work," and yet I had seen people of notoriety that had successfully traded along those lines. In addition, it was mathematical. In addition to that, it suited me because it was more long term in nature as opposed to trying to worry about what happened the last hour in the market. I was a busy guy, I didn't have the time to mess with what happened in the last hour. I was in the early stages. I was still working as an engineer trying to do stuff on a part-time basis, trying to get an MBA, trying to build a house out in the woods that I custom designed myself.

There was a lot on my plate in my 20s and 30s. I felt I had to try to be very efficient and trend following was a way of making sure that I always captured every major trend. As I told you before, in some years as little as two or three trades would be the difference at Trendstat between making money that year and breaking even. So you had to capture every one of those big ones.

Trend following would always mathematically capture a very large move. It couldn't fail to do that, and that gave me the reassurance that that's what I was going for. All this other stuff that you do every day— little losses, the two-thirds of the time that you lose money—that's all a lot of work to get you nowhere.

Aaron: Do you find that the structure of trends has changed from, say, 10, 20 years ago to how they are now? Is it fair to say that trends might have been much cleaner cut back then and in today's market the trends tend to jump around a lot more?

Tom: It could be. I frankly haven't taken the time to try to do that kind of analysis in recent years. I would say that there is some choppiness out there and a lot of it could be driven by shorter-term computer action. But the way I like to think of the trading world that I have observed over the last three or four decades is that that the use of computers has sped up everything. I think the whole world in trading can now move, say, a few billion shares. Whereas, back when I came out of college in '74, a really good day at the end of the '73/'74 bear market, which lasted two years, was 10 million shares on the New York Stock Exchange. To put that in perspective, SPY trades hundreds of millions of shares all by itself. One instrument trades literally 20, 30, 40 times the amount that the entire New York Stock Exchange traded in '74 because they were doing it all by hand. There were tickets, there were telephone calls, there was a lot of running around and very inefficient approaches to doing everything.

Now you can do all that a lot faster and you can even tell your computer to make the decision faster, to transmit it faster. Everything's set up. So I don't know that the trends have changed all that much, but they probably happen a lot faster.

To me what constitutes a full trend is a large cycle of human psychology when it comes to investing. There's the "I don't want to ever get into the stock market again" stage. Then there's the stage where stocks start going up, but "I don't trust it," and then they go up a little further and "I don't know, maybe I should get into this?" Then you start hearing about it at cocktail parties, and you almost have to buy in at that point, and by the time you get around to doing it, it's actually at the high and about ready to reverse that psychology and go the other way.

These days, a lot of that psychological shift from depression to euphoria seems to happen a lot quicker. We've got telecommunications, we have logs and all sorts of news coming to our phones. So we know what's the latest on the Greek crisis, and what the Prime Minister is going to say and there're 25 people analyzing what he's going to say or what he's not going to say. It's compressing. In the old days you had to wait till *The Wall Street Journal* showed up to get some of this stuff. Nowadays, everything's electronic, everything can react quickly.

Aaron: You observed that there seems to be an obsession with predicting rather than being in the now amongst many traders today. Would you like to expand on this?

Tom: When people find out I used to be a trader, even at friends' parties or wherever, they start talking about investing. It's something that affects almost everybody. You'll get in conversations about, "Well, what do you think is going to happen to the dollar? What do you think is going to happen here? What do you think the government is going to do here?"

I can carry on an intelligent conversation. I used to have to know what countries were doing with their currencies and I'd be thoroughly well-read on that. If for no other reason than during a client interview where some major bank is trying to hire me to manage their currencies, that I can speak intelligently about various economies and at least appear— even though it has nothing to do whatsoever with my trading—to be intelligent and knowledgeable about various economic things that are going on around the world.

I have continued to do that. I've followed this whole euro thing and the Greece thing with fascination, because in 1997 when people were interviewing me I absolutely, 100%, with no punches pulled at all, said that the euro is a dumb idea and it will never last long term. It cannot. You can't base all sorts of different political systems into a single currency that's based on a whole bunch of different balance sheets. It won't happen. Somebody's going to cheat; somebody's not going to pull their weight. Other people are going to be getting the shaft on it and having to pay for the people who weren't doing it right, and that's what you're seeing now.

Some of the German people have got to be getting fed up with the others, too—the places like Greece and Italy, Portugal, Spain, and other places that seem to be socialist and debt ridden and don't seem to be able to get their act together at all, financially speaking. How long are you going to run that until you just say, "I've had enough" and then you break it apart again?

I've always thought it was a dumb idea. Well, the prediction of that is all good and fine, but in reality, to trade, all I care about in trading is where should my portfolio be positioned this moment, right now, period. Nothing more than that. You don't know what tomorrow's going to bring, you don't care a whole lot about what yesterday brought because that's already gone and never coming back.

You really need to concentrate on looking at your portfolio. I've heard Paul Tudor Jones say this on occasion, where he likes to start each day assuming that all his positions are wrong, like he's starting all over again, and he's reanalyzing where does he want to be right now. If he assumes that everything is wrong, he's critical then about every position. He tries to decide, "No, I do like that position. I want to hold it for another day." I think that's trying to force himself to be in the now and that's a good thing.

The only thing you have control of as a trader is buying or selling right now. You can't buy three weeks from now; there's no point to that.

Aaron: You have talked before about a coin-flip concept—you referred to how entries are less important than money management and good risk management and exits.

Tom: I did the random study. I took the computers and I had them create a random number generator. I applied this to around eight markets and at the end of every day, if I didn't have a position, I would put in a position using the random number generator. Somebody else in Austria replicated it with 20 markets. It came out the same. In fact, they might have even made more money than I did, but we were all slightly positive—not robustly positive, just slightly.

What it came down to is the same concept I mentioned already. If you trade all year long, two or three trades are the difference between making a very nice profit versus breaking even. You must be in on those trades some place. Then once you get in on those trades, you need to let them run and mature and bring you those very large profits that you seek.

A random number generator that simply says, "Okay, I don't care which way I go. The markets could go down a lot, they could go up a lot. I'm just going to flip a coin and, whatever it says, the next morning I'm going to buy the open or sell the open as the case may be."

But once I get that new position, I have to try to assume it's the next really, really big winner that I've got, so I need to trail my stops at a logical level, give it enough room to move, to be safely restricting the risk but at the same time giving it room for normal movement. So things like average true range, things like breakouts on charts, all of those types of things, depending on how sophisticated you want to be about it, could come into play to give the market normal movement, but to allow that profit to keep building and building and building over the long run for that one trade.

As soon as it hits that stop, that tells you that trend was not the one you were looking for—it was not that major trade that would pay its way for the portfolio to be successful for you.

So what you'd end up with is you'd be out of the market and flip it again. The random number is going to give you 50% buys, and 50% sells. It isn't going to be long until you're going to match up with that big trend that's going to make all the money for you, and that's how you're going to make the slight amounts of profit for the year.

You're going to have lots of losers, you're going to have some gainers, and you're going to have one or two or three very, very large gainers, and those are the ones you have to be in on, and a random number generator will give you those.

Aaron: Psychology is probably the most important aspect of profitable trading. Why do you believe this to be the most important aspect?

Tom: I would say good trading falls into three different things that have to happen. The first one, which everybody spends all their time on, is the buy and sell decision. You have to have a way to say, "This is how I would buy or sell a market, a stock or whatever it is that you're trading." Second, you have to answer the question of, "How much should I buy and what types of instruments should I buy?" I call that whole area the sort of portfolio management, risk management, volatility management area. You have to be successful at that too.

The third area—the most important one in my opinion, and the one that a lot of people spend the least amount of time thinking about—is your own psychology. Even in the case of fully automated Trendstat back in the day, I as a human being had the ultimate power as the owner of Trendstat to go in and pull the plug on the computer, override it or do whatever because I owned the company, 100%.

If my psychology and my knowledge of what we were doing wasn't in good shape, and I wasn't comfortable with what we had created, then the first time I go through a drawdown I'm going to start second guessing myself and all those computers, and I'm going to start telling my computer staff we need a whole new way of doing things, and let's go research this latest hot strategy that seems to have made 50% last year. I could go buy black boxes or build black boxes, what's the difference, and keep switching in trading and fail time after time after time because my psychology wasn't right.

So even though I was automated, you still have to have a good, balanced mind about what you're doing. There's a good example that I've heard Doctor Van Tharp talk about. Good trading is following your strategy that day. It is not whether you made money or lost money that day; it's simply following your strategy. That's a very profound thing. It hit me a long, long time ago when I heard him say that. I thought, "Yeah, that's perfect. That's exactly what I do every day." That's why he and I worked together. For a few years, I helped him out with some seminars he was doing and I found it fascinating to meet a lot of people around the world. We had a good time doing them until my schedule got so busy it got unreasonable to do them any more.

But that was a very substantive and smart way of putting it. Good trading is following your strategy. Good trading isn't making money and bad trading losing money. Good strategy development is what you need to do and, once you have that strategy, you need to follow it and to actually execute it.

The time to change your strategy isn't in the heat of the moment halfway through the trading session when your particular position has gone against you by 3%, and you're not sure whether you should pull the plug on it or not. You should have already figured that out and it should be just blindly done. When you're out on a position and the markets are closed, if you want to sit back and think about what just went on and try to come up with a better way, all good and fine.

I'm not saying that anybody shouldn't be constantly striving. I was sitting here just today completely mesmerized by some stock research that I was doing. So I still am doing it here at 62 years old, retired. I think you do have to keep working and getting better. But you have to stick to whatever it is that you're coming up with unless you can figure out a better way.

A lot of people don't do that. They pull the plug on it or even buy the black box. Six months later they throw it out again and they change everything they're doing. They're adding so many layers of filters.

I've had people via Facebook give me a message and ask me questions and I'll say, "Tell me what you're doing, and I'll see if I can react to it." They'll go into this involved explanation of all the different filtering, and they only do it if the ADX is X, and on and on and on. I'm wondering how they ever get a trade to happen, they've got so many filters on the thing. They're trying to achieve perfection. It's so complicated that it's probably not workable, and they're likely to miss those two or three very large trades that are going to pay the way because they've filtered those trades out somehow.

I encourage people to really understand their own mind. I think some people are a little more cut out for trading than others. Sometimes the extremely cerebral, highly intellectual, brilliant people, who view themselves as smarter than everybody else, have a hard time with trading because they just know too much. Some of the best traders—if you look at some of the long traders, the people that have come off the streets that really don't know a whole lot about investing at all, certainly don't have an MBA or anything—are successful traders because they find something that works and then stick to it. They don't let the markets beat them up because they don't really have that mental side of them that wants to analyze and theoretically understand everything out there. They just want to make some money and go home, so that's what they do.

Everybody needs to study their own psychology and try to ask themselves what they could be doing to balance themselves out more, so that when they're doing actual trading functions they can stay in the now, they can analyze where they want to be, be fairly unemotional about it and react quickly. That's really what good trading is. That's psychology.

You can do all the work you want but if don't have the psychology, that key third area, you'll never execute those first two areas of trading.

Aaron: When Jack Schwager interviewed you for *The New Market Wizards*, he actually dubbed you as "Mr. Serenity" because of your cool, calm and collected style of trading. How were you able to actually achieve this and maintain this evenly keeled mindset, even through times of drawdown?

Tom: I've asked myself that question a number of times. The only thing I can think of that seems to play in my mind about history and my life, looking back, is that I was always so goddarn busy doing so many things that didn't involve sitting by a phone or in front of a quote machine. I had so many varied interests that were outside the markets. I've run into people that in the middle of the night wake up and they want to see a quote machine down by their bed to know what the euro's doing tonight. That's obsessive to me.

I like to call friends. I'm going to cook dinner tonight. I love helping other traders. Yesterday I was pruning my front yard. I love to do an Italian landscape scheme where everything's flowering. I hand prune all my bushes and trees myself. There're so many things for me to fill up my day that trading just becomes one of the many, many things. By doing that, it removes the attention to my conscious brain from all the different events of the world. The Greek crisis is doing this, and, "Oh my God; gold's up $10," and all these different things that go on that could capture your mind and all of a sudden pull you down a psychological hole.

Because I was so busy, because I allowed the computers to do their things, because I spent time programming those computers to do what I wanted them to do, and I knew they were doing that, it gave me that peace of mind to wonder what I was going to cook for dinner that night, to concentrate on my golf game, or have fun vacations in some place. I didn't have to be obsessed with every day reading the paper, reading quote machines, looking at the charts, agonizing over everything.

A lot of traders are so caffeinated. Including Jack, I believe, back in the day when he interviewed me—New York, fast, go-go personality, constantly driving. A lot of the *Market Wizards* that he interviewed, some of whom aren't around anymore, were pretty fast high-risk guys in the end, and some of them blew up and didn't make it over the long run.

By comparison, I was pretty boring. Where I was unusual was my kind of systematic, keep it simple, don't get stressed out over it approach. I think that appealed to Jack in a way because he sort of wanted to adapt some of that for himself. It was a fun process. I enjoy Jack; he's a great guy.

Aaron: You spoke about viewing your life like a movie. What did you mean by this and how does this have a positive impact on your life and, more specifically, a positive impact on your trading?

Tom: If you watch a movie, the scene that is on the screen right at that moment is always going to be the now. You are allowed to guess where the plot's going; you might guess right, you might guess wrong. It's kind of like the markets. You might think it's going to go up more, but it might not. But you know what you're looking at right there, because it's on the screen right now.

If you pay attention to right now, then you can allow a horror flick to horrify you or an emotional film to make you cry, or a comedy to make you laugh at that moment, because you paid attention, and there was a joke there and you said, "That's funny."

Your emotions can go all over the place, but you aren't attaching yourself. You know that it's a film; it's there for entertainment. You still have your own life, your own beliefs, your own everything inside you. I like to think of the markets and life as sort of a movie. You kind of know which way the movie's headed, but life throws you a lot of unexpected turns. So do the markets. You just have to look at it and say, "Okay, that was interesting. Now what are we going to do?" How do you react to it? What was your strategy supposed to do during that new information or new change in the conditions? It keeps you separated emotionally from the actual trade.

You can look at trading as a movie, rather than feel like trading is your life, and you're surrounded by the market in every way you turn and look. You wake up, and you go to the market, and you're checking the market before you go to sleep, and you've got your phone in front of you all day long. During lunch you're not carrying on conversations with people because you're worried about what's happening to the euro. That to me is not watching the movie. That would be kind of losing yourself in the middle of the movie.

Aaron: You've made a conscious effort throughout your years as a money manager, and even still to this day during retirement, that your way of trading was designed to fit the lifestyle that you wanted to live and not the other way around.

Tom: I get a lot of calls and messages from people on Facebook and Twitter asking how I trade. I hate to be rude, but I feel like saying to them: Why do you care? You should be designing what you do for you. Why would you want to do what I am doing? I have a different net worth, I have a different expertise level, I have different computer equipment than you do. I may have different legal restrictions in terms of the markets I can trade.

Some people from India are asking me questions. I have no idea what the Indian stock market looks like, or what the regulations are, or what the brokerage conditions there are. I've never, ever traded in Indian stocks; don't plan to lately unless something changes. I just don't know anything about it. So why are you trying to apply what I'm doing to your life? It'd be better for you to be developing what it is that you want to do on your own.

That's exactly what I've done. I'm in retirement. I do spend a little time trading every day. Today, as I just mentioned a while back, I got immersed in a little bit of stock research because I had some ideas I wanted to explore. I didn't come to any profound conclusions sadly. But it did certainly burn up a couple of hours of my day. Nothing's changed—tomorrow I'll do the same thing I did today in terms of trading— but it gives me something to think about.

I can go on vacation and take my PC along and maybe spend 20 minutes to half an hour a day on my trading; that's the most time I'm willing to part with on vacation. If I can get it all done in a short amount of time—they have an internet connection on our cruise ship, let's say, or wherever—I can get my job done every day, continue to trade my strategy. It's designed around me being able to do that.

I find so many people looking at systems and strategies when they have full-time jobs and I'm thinking, "How are you going to do that with a full-time job? You're supposed to be out there talking to customers or building widgets. How are you going to be able to focus and pull it off? You're going to miss trades, you do not have capital to diversify it." There're lots and lots of problems you see right out of the gate.

The biggest thing I find with a lot of people is capital. They want to start from nothing and they'll tell me they've got $2,000 and ask how they start trading futures contracts. I scratch my head on that one because I have to admit I started with about a $2,000 or a $3,000 account, had no clue what I was doing, and I'm sure glad that I figured it out because I ended up losing money for four years and it took a long while to get to where break-even occurred. But as I got larger in size, more diversified, and got better risk control, volatility control, it all came together.

I think trying to do all that with $2,000 is mathematically impossible. So people are under-capitalized, they don't have a knowledge of what they're facing, and I think it's sad that they aren't thinking through, "What should I be doing to design something for me?" They should be thinking,

"How could I make my trading strategy my own, make it exclusively mine, make it suit my lifestyle, my capital, my resources, my expertise levels?" They're going to be so much more capable of getting that psychological sweet spot of being able to stay in the now and do what they need to do because it's theirs.

They don't have to worry about what Tom's doing with his stuff, or what Michael Covel's doing with his stuff, or Jack Schwager with his stuff. It doesn't make any difference. It's only important what *I* should be doing with *my* stuff.

Aaron: It's clear that you're a big believer in taking full responsibility for all aspects of your life, so I'd love to hear your thoughts on why you feel so strongly about this.

Tom: It was empowering once I figured out that I was responsible for everything in my trading. The market is going to go through large ups, abrupt downs. It's going to have a lot of noise at times; it's going to be dull at other times. That's what markets do. You can't blame the market for your problems. You've got to take it on yourself and say, "What can I do to deal with all of what mankind's going to throw at me over my lifetime?" When you answer that question, you'll be developing a pretty good trading strategy that'll suit you.

As an example, Greece is in the news right now. Greece is not taking responsibility for its own mismanagement. There's this tendency among various factions of society today either to blame somebody else or to expect somebody else to take care of some of their problems. There's less and less self-responsibility in society today. I don't think that's leading us in the right direction at all. It seems to me that we're getting lots of governments around the world in trouble financially; more and more defaults.

Argentina's not looking so good; Venezuela's a disaster. The United States is spending way beyond its means. Sooner or later, this whole thing starts caving in. I don't know how the world reacts to that. It's going to end up being pretty messy because there're a lot of governments around the world that are going to be in trouble financially, and when people just stop giving them money through government bonds and loans, or they deflate or inflate their currency by just printing too much of it, people are going to suffer in those countries. It's going to get nasty if people don't take responsibility.

The whole thing about self-responsibility to me is it gives you a little peace of mind that you have the ability to do something about it, instead of having life throw things at you.

If you try to take responsibility for everything that happens, then you're going to be a little bit better at reacting and doing what's necessary to lead your life in a good way and make positive contributions to society, make positive contributions to your trading strategy. All of those things are going to be enhanced by self-responsibility.

Aaron: You like to say, "Enjoy the ride." You often end tweets with these three words, and while they're very simple, I feel like there's a deeper message here. Would you mind sharing that with us? What's the significance of this phrase?

Tom: The significance of it is a philosophical one. Life is like a ride; you get your ups and downs and unexpected surprises and all that, and in the end you're dead, so you might as well enjoy the ride.

I think people make too much of some things. I know all sorts of traders that can't quit because they're so addicted to it; they identify themselves as traders. They don't identify themselves as human beings that are fathers and husbands and neighbors to other people; they instead are just immersed in this thing called trading.

You could say the same thing about people who are teachers, people who are salesmen, people who install shades and blinds. There're all sorts of examples I can tell you about. I have friends who are well past normal retirement, but they just can't stop doing what they're doing because they identify with that. They haven't created an identity for themselves outside of that.

The enjoy the ride thing is just basically to look at life like a movie. Enjoy the ride, just like most movies; there're unexpected twists, and you laugh, and you're emotional, and you should be able to enjoy all that because life's short, and why not do that? There's no point in doing anything other than that, really. It's the same with the downs of the market—"Enjoy the ride."

Today, we had a down signal come in at the time we're doing this interview, it was just midday. I saw the hedges go on and so I got on

Twitter and I put it out to everybody. I get five new people following me. It gets shared all over the place, and it's kind of weird from my standpoint. In reality, I had a down day today monetarily. I didn't go down as much as the market did, so that was good. I guess I buffered a little bit of risk. If the market continues down, I'll look really good; if the market turns around tomorrow and goes up, I'll look stupid again, and that's fine because I'm enjoying the ride.

I'm going to go work on a beautiful dinner for tonight, and I'm going to enjoy myself during the evening, and I'm not going to think about it a lot. Tomorrow I'll do the same thing again, and I'll continue to enjoy the ride.

About the Author

MICHAEL Covel searches. He digs. He goes behind the curtain to reveal a state of mind the system does not want you in.

Characterized as essential and required reading, Michael teaches beginners to seasoned pros how to generate profits with straightforward and repeatable rules. He is best known for popularizing the counterintuitive and controversial trading strategy, trend following.

An avowed entrepreneur, Michael is the author of five books, including the international bestseller, *Trend Following*, and his investigative narrative, *Turtle Trader*. Fascinated by secretive traders that have quietly generated spectacular returns for seven decades, those going against the investment orthodoxy of buy and hope, he has uncovered astonishing insights about the right way to think, develop, and execute trend following systems.

Michael's perspectives have garnered international acclaim and have earned him invitations with a host of organizations: China Asset Management, GIC Private Limited (a Singapore sovereign wealth fund), BM&F Bovespa, the Managed Funds Association, Bank of China Investment Management, the Market Technicians Association, and multiple hedge funds and mutual funds. He also has the distinction of having interviewed five Nobel Prize winners in economics, including Daniel Kahneman and Harry Markowitz; and he has been featured in major media outlets, including *The Wall Street Journal*, Bloomberg, CCTV, *The Straits Times*, and Fox Business.

Michael posts on Twitter, publishes a blog, and records his podcast weekly. His consulting clients include hedge funds, sovereign wealth funds, institutional investors, and individual traders in more than 70 countries. He splits his time between the United States and Asia.

www.trendfollowing.com

About Tom Basso

Tom Basso, currently retired, was CEO of Trendstat Capital Management, Inc., a Registered Investment and Commodity Trading Advisory (CTA) firm. He received an undergraduate degree in chemical engineering from Clarkson University and a Master's in Business Administration from Southern Illinois University. He has participated as an Arbitrator for the National Association of Securities Dealers and National Futures Association (NFA), and is a past Director on the NFA Board, representing one of four CTA/CPO seats on the board.

In addition, Tom served on the NFA's technology and standards sub-committee for three years. He served on the Board of Directors of the National Association of Active Investment Managers (NAIIM) and was a past director of CreaMiser, Inc., now a division of Dean Foods, which is the leading provider of bulk cream dispensing in the US. He was on the Management Committee of Lamp Technologies, a Dallas-based technology company specializing in back office outsourcing solutions for the futures and hedge fund industry. In 2019, Tom became Chairman of the Board of Standpoint Alternative Asset Management, which manages funds with a blend of managed futures and global equities. The fund is managed by Eric Crittenden and gives investors exposure to a single manager, multi-strategy, multi-market approach to investing.

His engineering, mathematical and computer background gave Tom the ability to develop a wide range of investment programs to take advantage of opportunities in the financial markets worldwide. He has authored *Panic Proof Investing*, which is dedicated to helping investors, and was one of the traders featured in *The New Market Wizards*, a book on successful traders written by Jack Schwager. His recent book, *Successful Traders Size Their Positions – Why and How?* has been a hit with traders worldwide attempting to manage their position sizes. At their peak, Trendstat managed $600 million for clients worldwide from Scottsdale, Arizona. Tom currently has created a website dedicated to traders: enjoytheride.world. He has been retired since 2003 and enjoys a variety of activities, including golf, writing, singing in a church choir, working out and helping traders through his retirement website, with books, videos, references, research, webinars, seminars and other helpful resources.

enjoytherideworld.odoo.com

Bibliography

Basso, Thomas F. "Adding Low Sharpe Ratio Investments Can Increase Your Sharpe Ratio." Trendstat Capital Management.

Basso, Thomas F. "Algorithmic Trading Is Getting A Bad Rap." Trendstat Capital Management, November 28, 2018.

Basso, Thomas F. "CTA Cycles – Surges follow the declines." Trendstat Capital Management, December 1999.

Basso, Thomas F. "Currency Investing – Increasing Net Worth While Protecting Net Wealth." Trendstat Capital Management.

Basso, Thomas F. "Good Trading Is Not Rocket Science." Trendstat Capital Management.

Basso, Thomas F. "Some Leverage is Good, Too Much is Dangerous." Trendstat Capital Management.

Basso, Thomas F. "Study of Time Spent in Trending and Sideways Markets." Trendstat Capital Management, March 1999.

Basso, Thomas F. "Ten Rules to Consider When Investing Your Money." Trendstat Capital Management.

Basso, Thomas F. "The ETR Comfort Ratio." Trendstat Capital Management.

Basso, Thomas F. "The Value Added of Asset Allocation Combined with Rebalancing." Trendstat Capital Management, May 12, 2000.

Basso, Thomas F. "Thoughts on Good Investing Psychology in the Midst of Turmoil." Trendstat Capital Management, September 17, 2001.

Basso, Thomas F. "Time Stocks Spent in Up, Down and Sideways Markets (2018 Update)." Trendstat Capital Management, October 2, 2018.

Basso, Thomas F. "Timing the Market Revisited." Trendstat Capital Management.

Covel, Michael, host. "Ep. 10: Tom Basso Interview with Michael Covel on Trend Following Radio." Trend Following Radio, April 25, 2012. http://trendfollowingradio.com/tom-basso-interview-trend-following-manifesto-with-michael-covel.

Covel, Michael, host. "Ep. 83: Tom Basso Interview #2 with Michael Covel on Trend Following Radio." Trend Following Radio, November 28, 2012. http://trendfollowingradio.com/tom-basso-interview-2-trend-following-manifesto-with-michael-covel.

Covel, Michael, host. "Ep. 200: Tom Basso Interview #3 with Michael Covel on Trend Following Radio." Trend Following Radio, January 10, 2014. http://trendfollowingradio.com/ep-200-tom-basso-interview-3-with-michael-covel-on-trend-following-radio.

Covel, Michael, host. "Ep. 306: Tom Basso Interview #4 with Michael Covel on Trend Following Radio." Trend Following Radio, January 1, 2015. http://trendfollowingradio.com/ep-306-tom-basso-interview-4-with-michael-covel-on-trend-following-radio.

Covel, Michael, host. "Ep. 700: Tom Basso Interview #4 with Michael Covel on Trend Following Radio." Trend Following Radio, October 8, 2018. http://trendfollowingradio.com/ep-700-tom-basso-interview-with-michael-covel-on-trend-following-radio.

Covel, Michael. *The Complete Turtle Trader*. New York: HarperCollins, 2009.

Covel, Michael. *The Little Book of Trading*. New Jersey: John Wiley & Sons, Inc., 2011.

Covel, Michael. *Trend Following 5th Edition*. New Jersey: Pearson Education, Inc., 2011.

Covel, Michael. *Trend Commandments*. New Jersey: John Wiley & Sons, Inc., 2017.

Fifield, Aaron, host. "Ep. 30: The logic of trend following, and how to improve your trader psychology with Market Wizard, Tom Basso." Chat With Traders, July 22, 2015. https://chatwithtraders.com/ep-030-tom-basso.

Lundell, Dean. "Guide to Becoming a CTA." Chicago Mercantile Exchange, 2004.

Appendix: Trend Following Podcast—Selected Interviews with Michael Covel

My trend following podcast has generated over 10 million listens across 1000+ episodes. Please enjoy all episodes on iTunes and at www.trendfollowing.com.

Here is a list of selected highlights from among the interviews.

Ep. 892: Gary Hamel—Gary P. Hamel is an American management consultant. He is a founder of Strategos, an international management consulting firm based in Chicago.

Ep. 890: David Cote—David M. Cote is an American businessman. He was CEO of Honeywell from 2002–2017.

Ep. 874: Mark Victor Hansen and Crystal Dwyer Hansen—Mark Victor Hansen is best known as the founder and co-creator of the *Chicken Soup for the Soul* book series.

Ep. 857: Jack Canfield—Jack Canfield is best known as the co-creator of the *Chicken Soup for the Soul* book series.

Ep. 841: Tom Golisano—Thomas Golisano is an American billionaire businessman, philanthropist, and author. He is the founder of Paychex.

Ep. 829: Steve Blank—Steve Blank is a Silicon Valley entrepreneur recognized for developing the customer development method that launched the lean startup movement.

Ep. 827: Chris Ryan—Chris Ryan is the *New York Times* bestselling co-author of *Sex at Dawn*.

Ep. 824: Robert Greifeld—Robert Greifeld is former CEO and Chairman of Nasdaq.

Ep. 823: Joseph Pine—Joseph Pine is author of *Welcome to the Experience Economy*.

Ep. 815: Mark Minervini—Mark Minervini is author of *Mindset Secrets for Winning*.

Ep. 814: Gregory Zuckerman—Gregory Zuckerman is the author of *The Man Who Solved the Market: How Jim Simons Launched the Quant Revolution*.

Ep. 808: Niels Kaastrup-Larsen—Niels Kaastrup-Larsen is Managing Director of DUNN Capital (Europe).

Ep. 807: Laurie Santos—Laurie Santos is a professor of psychology and cognitive science at Yale University.

Ep. 806: Vitaliy Katsenelson—Vitaliy Katsenelson, CFA, is Chief Investment Officer at Investment Management Associates.

Ep. 804: Larry Hite—Larry Hite was the founding principal and Managing Director of Mint Investment Management Company.

Ep. 803: Rita McGrath—Rita McGrath is a globally recognized expert on strategy, innovation, and growth with an emphasis on corporate entrepreneurship.

Ep. 789: Scott Kupor—Scott Kupor is the managing partner of Andreessen Horowitz.

Ep. 773: Esther Wojcicki—Esther Wojcicki is known as the Godmother of Silicon Valley.

Ep. 767: Steve Burns—Steve Burns took to blogging and social media by founding New Trader U in 2011.

Ep. 739: Peter Borish—Peter Borish is chief strategist of Quad Capital. He also is a founding member of the Robin Hood Foundation.

Ep. 723: Harold de Boer—Harold de Boer is a trend following legend with a consistent track record dating back to the 1980s.

Ep. 710: Peter Boettke—Peter Boettke is an economist of the Austrian School. He is currently an economics and philosophy professor at George Mason University.

Ep. 705: Howard Marks—Howard Marks is an investor, writer and author of *Mastering the Market Cycle: Getting the Odds on Your Side*. He co-founded Oaktree Capital Management.

Ep. 701: Jeffrey Gitomer—Jeffrey Gitomer is an author, professional speaker, and business trainer. He is best known for *The Little Red Book of Selling*.

Ep. 697: Jerry Parker—Jerry Parker is the founder of Chesapeake Capital and was one of the original TurtleTraders trained by Richard Dennis.

Ep. 694: Ken Kocienda—Ken Kocienda was a software engineer/designer at Apple for over 15 years and is the author of *Creative Selection: Inside Apple's Design Process During the Golden Age of Steve Jobs*.

Ep. 685: Lawrence Krauss—Lawrence Krauss is a theoretical physicist and cosmologist, professor at Arizona State University, director of its Origins Project and author of bestselling books *The Physics of Star Trek* and *A Universe from Nothing*.

Ep. 677: Mark Blyth—Mark Blyth is a political scientist from Scotland and a professor of international political economy at Brown University.

Ep. 669: Harvey Silverglate—Harvey Silverglate is an events attorney with 51 years of experience practicing in courts throughout the country. He is also author of *Three Felonies A Day: How the Feds Target the Innocent*.

Ep. 666: Aaron Brown—Aaron Brown is a finance practitioner, expert on risk management and gambling, frequent speaker at professional and academic conferences, author of *Red-Blooded Risk* and *The Poker Face of Wall Street*, and co-author of *A World of Chance*.

Ep. 655: Roy Baumeister—Roy Baumeister is a social psychologist known for his work on the self, social rejection, belongingness, sexuality, sex differences, self-control, self-esteem, self-defeating behaviors, motivation, aggression, consciousness and free will.

Ep. 653: Alexander Elder—Alexander Elder has written some of the most popular trading books of the last 30 years.

Ep. 640: Alison Gopnik—Alison Gopnik is an American professor of psychology and affiliate professor of philosophy at the University of California, Berkeley.

Ep. 639: Martin Bergin and James Dailey – Martin Bergin is the President and owner of DUNN Capital Management.

Ep. 637: Oliver Hart—Oliver Hart is a British-born American economist, and currently the Andrew E. Furer Professor of Economics at Harvard University. He received the Nobel Memorial Prize in Economic Sciences in 2016 for his work on contract theory.

Ep. 633: William Damon—William Damon is a Professor of Education at the Stanford Graduate School of Education, Director of the Stanford Center on Adolescence, and senior fellow at Stanford University's Hoover Institution.

Ep. 629: Annie Duke—Annie Duke is a poker player, author, decision-making expert, and cognitive scientist. Her latest book is *Thinking in Bets: Making Smarter Decisions When You Don't Have All the Facts.*

Ep. 627: Charles Faulkner—Charles Faulkner is an author, trader, and international expert on modeling the knowledge and performance of exceptional individuals.

Ep. 617: Ken Blanchard—Ken Blanchard is an author and management expert. His writing career spans over 60 books, with his most successful being *The One Minute Manager,* selling over 13 million copies.

Ep. 615: Robin Hanson—Robin Hanson is an associate professor of economics at George Mason University and a research associate at the Future of Humanity Institute of Oxford University.

Ep. 593: Scott Galloway—Scott Galloway is a professor at New York University Stern School of Business teaching brand strategy and digital marketing.

Ep. 591: Jeffrey Tucker—Jeffrey Tucker is an American economics writer of the Austrian School, an advocate of anarcho-capitalism and Bitcoin, and has authored seven books.

Ep. 587: Robert Sutton—Robert Sutton is Professor of Management science at the Stanford Engineering School and researcher in the field of Evidence-based management. He is also the best-selling author of *The No Asshole Rule.*

Ep. 586: Jason Calacanis—Jason Calacanis is a venture capitalist, entrepreneur, angel investor, author and blogger, and has years of perspective when it comes to investing in start-ups.

Ep. 583: Richard Clarke—Richard Clarke is co-author of *Warnings: Finding Cassandras to Stop Catastrophes.* He was also the former National Coordinator for Security, Infrastructure Protection and Counter-terrorism for the United States.

Ep. 575: Tyler Cowen—Tyler Cowen is author of *The Complacent Class: The Self-Defeating Quest for the American Dream.*

Ep. 573: Jon Gordon—Jon Gordon is an author and speaker on leadership, culture, sales, and teamwork. His latest book is *The Power of Positive Leadership*.

Ep. 569: Andrew Lo—Andrew Lo is author of *Adaptive Markets: Financial Evolution at the Speed of Thought*. He is also the Charles E. and Susan T. Harris Professor of Finance at MIT.

Ep. 564: John Force—John Force is an American NHRA drag racer. He is a 16-time champion and his team has 18 championships under them. John is one of the most dominant drag racers in the sport with over 144 career victories.

Ep. 561: Jeff Goins—Jeff Goins is author of *Real Artists Don't Starve: Timeless Strategies for Thriving in the New Creative Age*.

Ep. 555: Denise Shull—Denise Shull is a performance and decision coach to traders and athletes. She is well known for her effectiveness in assessing performance under high-pressure situations.

Ep. 551: Jack Schwager—Jack Schwager is author of the *Market Wizards* series.

Ep. 543: Cass R. Sunstein—Cass R. Sunstein is the Robert Walmsley University Professor at Harvard Law School.

Ep. 533: Donald Hoffman—Donald Hoffman is a cognitive scientist at UC Irvine. He studies how our visual perception, guided by millions of years of natural selection, authors every aspect of our everyday reality.

Ep. 531: Mark Rzepczynski—Mark Rzepczynski is the CEO of AMPHI Capital Management and has a deep knowledge of trading, especially trend following trading.

Ep. 516: Wesley Gray—Wesley Gray served as a Captain in the United States Marine Corps and taught as a finance professor at Drexel University.

Ep. 507: Lanny Bassham—Lanny Bassham went to the 1976 Olympics and won the gold medal in rifle shooting.

Ep. 489: Chris Voss—Chris Voss is the author of *Never Split The Difference: Negotiating As If Your Life Depended On It*. Chris is a former international hostage negotiator for the FBI.

Ep. 487: Robert Cialdini—Robert Cialdini is best known for writing *Influence: The Psychology of Persuasion*.

Ep. 459: Tucker Max—Tucker Max is an author and entrepreneur.

Ep. 455: Ryan Holiday—Ryan Holiday is an entrepreneur and author of numerous books, including *Ego is the Enemy*.

Ep. 437: Anders Ericsson—Anders Ericsson is author of *Peak: Secrets from the New Science of Expertise.*

Ep. 435: Steven Pinker—Steven Pinker is Johnstone Family Professor in the Department of Psychology at Harvard University.

Ep. 431: Bill Bonner—Bill Bonner is author of *Hormegeddon: How Too Much Of A Good Thing Leads To Disaster.*

Ep. 429: Jim Rogers—Jim Rogers is a famed American investor based in Singapore. He was co-founder of the Quantum Fund

Ep. 425: Philip Tetlock—Philip Tetlock is the author of *Superforecasting: The Art and Science of Prediction.*

Ep. 423: Angus Deaton—Angus Deaton was awarded the Nobel Memorial Prize in 2015 for his work in economic sciences and analysis on consumption, poverty and welfare.

Ep. 419: Mebane Faber—Mebane Faber is an author, blogger, and portfolio manager with Cambria Investment Management.

Ep. 401: Ben Carlson—Ben Carlson is the Director of Institutional Asset Management at Ritholtz Wealth Management.

Ep. 396: Kathleen Eisenhardt—Kathleen Eisenhardt is co-author of the bestselling book *Simple Rules.* She is also the Co-Director of the Stanford Technology Ventures Program.

Ep. 391: Charles Poliquin—Charles Poliquin is recognized as one of the world's most successful strength coaches and has coached Olympic to professional athletes.

Ep. 385: Paul Slovic—Paul Slovic is president of Decision Research and a professor of psychology at the University of Oregon.

Ep. 373: Lasse Pedersen—Lasse Pedersen is a finance professor at Copenhagen Business School, principal at AQR Capital Management, and author of book *Efficiently Inefficient.*

Ep. 363: Blair Hull—Blair Hull got his start playing blackjack in Nevada casinos, and later moved onto trading. He founded his investment firm Hull Investments in 1999.

Ep. 355: Ed Seykota—Ed Seykota is an author, trader and was originally profiled in the classic book *The Market Wizards.*

Ep. 345: Spyros Makridakis—Spyros Makridakis is the Rector of the Neapolis University of Pafos NUP and an Emeritus Professor of Decision Sciences at INSEAD as well as the University of Piraeus.

Ep. 344: Martin Lueck—Martin Lueck is the Research Director and President of Aspect Capital. He was originally with Adam, Harding and Lueck Limited (AHL), which he co-founded with Michael Adam and David Harding.

Ep. 340 Tim Ferriss—Tim Ferriss is an author, blogger and motivational speaker known for his bestselling books.

Ep. 336: Colin Camerer—Colin Camerer is an American behavioral economist and a Robert Kirby Professor of Behavioral Finance and Economics at the California Institute of Technology (Caltech).

Ep. 331: Douglas Emlen—Douglas Emlen is a professor at the University of Montana. He authored *Animal Weapons: The Evolution of Battle*.

Ep. 324: David Stockman—David Stockman has been a businessman, a Congressman, and Director of the Office of Management and Budget under President Ronald Reagan.

Ep. 319: Salem Abraham—Salem Abraham is the President of Abraham Trading Company with a 27-year track record.

Ep. 318: Christopher Chabris—Christopher Chabris is an author, American research psychologist, Associate Professor of Psychology and co-director of the Neuroscience Program at Union College.

Ep. 315 Michael Mauboussin—Michael Mauboussin is an author, investment strategist in the financial services industry and professor at the Columbia Graduate School of Business, and serves on the board of trustees at the Sante Fe Institute.

Ep. 313: Jean-Philippe Bouchaud—Jean-Philippe Bouchaud is founder and Chairman of Capital Fund Management (CFM) and professor of physics at École polytechnique.

Ep. 309 Mark Mobius—Mark Mobius, PhD, is executive chairman of Templeton Emerging Markets Group.

Ep. 305: Mark Manson—Mark Manson is an author and personal development consultant. Manson wrote the international bestseller *The Subtle Art of Not Giving a F*ck*.

Ep. 297: Gabriele Oettingen—Gabriele Oettingen is an author and Professor of Psychology at New York University and the University of Hamburg.

Ep. 296: Ewan Kirk—Ewan Kirk is the head of Cantab Capital and has brought his firm from $30 million AUM in 2006 to over $5 billion today.

Ep. 295: Gerd Gigerenzer—Gerd Gigerenzer is director of the Center for Adaptive Behavior and Cognition (ABC) at the Max Planck Institute for Human Development and director of the Harding Center for Risk Literacy.

Ep. 291: Steven Kotler—Steven Kotler is an American bestselling author, journalist, and entrepreneur. His articles have appeared in over 70 publications.

Ep. 287: Toby Crabel—Toby Crabel is founder of Crabel Capital Management.

Ep. 286: Alex Greyserman—Alex Greyserman is an author and Chief Scientist at managed futures firm ISAM. He is also a professor at Columbia University.

Ep. 285: Anthony Todd—Anthony Todd is the CEO of Aspect Capital, one of the most successful managed futures/trend following firms.

Ep. 284: Jason Fried—Jason Fried is the founder and CEO of Basecamp (formerly 37Signals). He is also the co-author of the book *Rework*.

Ep. 274: Guy Kawasaki—Guy Kawasaki is the chief evangelist of Canva, an online graphic design tool. Formerly, he was an advisor to the Motorola business unit of Google and chief evangelist of Apple.

Ep. 269: Robert Aumann—Robert Aumann received the Nobel Memorial Prize in Economic Sciences in 2005 for his work on conflict and cooperation through game-theory analysis.

Ep. 265: Leo Melamed—Leo Melamed is a pioneer of financial futures, currencies, and stock indexes. He became Chairman of the Chicago Mercantile Exchange in 1969.

Ep. 264: John H. Cochrane—John H. Cochrane is the AQR Capital Management Distinguished Service Professor of Finance at the University of Chicago Booth School of Business.

Ep. 263: Meir Statman—Meir Statman is a professor of finance at Santa Clara University and a behavioral finance expert. His acclaimed book is titled *What Investors Really Want*.

Ep. 260: Sally Hogshead—Sally Hogshead is an American speaker, author, former advertising executive, as well as the CEO of Fascinate, Inc.

Ep. 254: William Poundstone—William Poundstone is the author of *Fortune's Formula*, a book about the Kelly criterion.

Ep. 252: Ben Hunt—Ben Hunt is the creator of Epsilon Theory and inspiration behind Second Foundation Partners, which he co-founded with Rusty Guinn in June 2018.

Ep. 244: Walter Williams—Walter Williams is an American economist, commentator, and academic. He is the John M. Olin Distinguished Professor of Economics at George Mason University.

Ep. 235: Harry Markowitz—Harry Markowitz is considered the founder of modern finance and a Nobel Prize winner.

Ep. 223: Marc Faber—Marc Faber is editor and publisher of "The Gloom, Boom & Doom Report".

Ep. 212: Daniel Kahneman—Daniel Kahneman has been called the most important psychologist alive today. Kahneman is the 2002 winner of the Nobel Memorial Prize in Economic Sciences.

Ep. 211: John Bollinger—John Bollinger is responsible for a technical indicator: Bollinger Bands.

Ep. 197: Jack Horner—Jack Horner is a world-renowned paleontologist. He was the technical advisor for all of the *Jurassic Park* films.

Ep. 194: Dan Ariely—Dan Ariely is a professor of psychology and behavioral economics at Duke. He has a bestseller titled *Predictably Irrational*.

Ep. 178: Vernon Smith—Vernon Smith is a professor of economics at Chapman University in Orange, California. He also shared the 2002 Nobel Memorial Prize in Economic Sciences with Daniel Kahneman.

Ep. 168 Larry Williams—Larry Richard Williams is an American author, stock and commodity trader, and politician from the state of Montana.

Ep. 164 Richard Noble—Richard Noble is a Scottish entrepreneur who held the land-speed record between 1983 and 1997.

Ep. 126: James Altucher—James Altucher is an author, blogger, and entrepreneur.

Ep. 85: Barry Ritholtz—Barry Ritholtz is an author (*Bailout Nation*), newspaper columnist, blogger, equities analyst, television commentator, and Chairman and CIO of Ritholtz Wealth Management.

Listen to all episodes at www.trendfollowing.com.

I want to give a big shout out to Michelle Murphy. Michelle has helped me on three books and I'm forever indebted to her for all of her hard work.

Every owner of a physical copy of this edition of

Trend
Following
Mindset

can download the eBook for free direct from us at
Harriman House, in a DRM-free format that can be read
on any eReader, tablet or smartphone.

Simply head to:

ebooks.harriman-house.com/trendfollowingmindset

to get your copy now.